A GLORIOUS AGE IN AFRICA

A GLORIOUS AGE IN AFRICA

THE STORY OF THREE GREAT AFRICAN EMPIRES

Daniel Chu and
Elliott Skinner, Ph.D.

Illustrated by Moneta Barnett

Africa World Press, Inc.

Africa World Press, Inc.

First Africa World Press edition, 1990
Second Printing, 1991
Third Printing, 1992
Fourth Printing, 1995
Fifth Printing, 1996

First published by Doubleday & Company 1963

Cover Design by Ife Nii Owoo

Library of Congress Catalog Card Number: 90-80150

ISBN: 0-86543-166-3 Cloth
0-86543-167-1 Paper

CONTENTS

INTRODUCTION

The French representative in the Moroccan town of Fez could not believe his eyes, or ears. Before him stood a man dressed in dirty rags. This man had stumbled out of the desert on a hot August day in 1828. He seemed more dead than alive.

Weak from hunger, badly sunburned, his whole body shaking from a deep cough, the man slowly told his strange story.

He said his name was René Caillie. He said he was twenty-nine years old, born in France. Then the man declared to the stunned French representative that he, René Caillie, had seen with his own eyes the fabled city of Timbuktu.

Timbuktu! How that name had teased Europeans for centuries! From the bits and pieces of information that had gotten to Europe, it was whispered that Timbuktu was a place of unbelievable riches—a place of gold, gold, and more gold!

But Timbuktu was hidden deep in the interior of West Africa. At that time Europeans thought of Africa as "the dark continent," a forbidding place of mystery. Practically all that Europeans knew about Africa had come secondhand from Arab sources.

In order to get some firsthand knowledge of the interior of Africa, the Geographical Society of Paris in the early nineteenth century offered a prize of 10,000 francs to the first European to find Timbuktu, and return alive to tell about it.

In 1827 René Caillie, a young Frenchman, left Senegal on the west coast of Africa to find Timbuktu. He had made careful preparations. Caillie had learned to speak Arabic and he pretended to be a Moslem. He had made up a new "life story" for himself.

Caillie would say that he was an Egyptian Moslem who had been captured and taken to France. He would explain that he was trying to get back to his own homeland.

Caillie thought that the best way to win the trust of the local African people, most of whom were Moslems, was to act like one of them. The disguise worked. He attached himself to a caravan headed for Timbuktu. Though ill with fever and reduced to begging because his funds were soon gone, he did reach Timbuktu in April 1828.

He stayed in Timbuktu about two weeks before joining another caravan, one which headed northward across the world's largest desert, the Sahara of North Africa. For Caillie the journey across the Sahara was filled with terrible hardships. In his disguise as a poor Moslem pilgrim, he was obliged to walk beside the animals of the caravan. Tormented by thirst and hunger, by the blazing sun of the days and the bitter cold of the nights, he survived on whatever handouts that he could beg. Somehow he dragged himself to Fez, and from there to Tangier for the return trip to France.

His journey had taken 538 days and covered 2812 miles, most of it on foot. Nevertheless René Caillie had completed his journey alive, just barely, but alive.

Caillie became an immediate sensation. He was hailed by scholars, honored by royalty, and rewarded with prizes and pensions. His achievement caused the same sort of excitement that a modern astronaut causes on return from a journey in outer space.

But what about the 10,000-franc question? Did Caillie find a city of gold in the midst of West Africa?

Well, not exactly. Caillie wrote, "I beheld only a group of mud-huts in the midst of a wide plain covered with yellowish sand. The sky was a glowing, livid red and everything seemed gloomy and silent."

Many people shared Caillie's disappointment. They began to doubt the stories of Timbuktu and its fabulous wealth. Indeed, the word Timbuktu came to mean a distant, unimportant place in the middle of nowhere.

But was the wealth of Timbuktu only an imaginary story? The answer to that is no.

Caillie had simply made his journey too late, perhaps 300 or 400 years too late. By the nineteenth century Timbuktu had long passed its golden age. Desert warriors had invaded and sacked the city repeatedly. When Caillie saw it, Timbuktu was a mere shadow of its former glory.

Since the trailblazing efforts of René Caillie and other explorers, historians and scientists have patiently sifted and probed to unlock the secrets of Africa's past. Through archaeological finds, through restudy of old manuscripts they have pieced together a story of a highly-developed West African civilization that has never been accorded the attention that it has deserved.

The work of scholars in our own century has ended all doubt of Timbuktu's place of importance in the course of world civilization. Timbuktu was a seat of power for fabulous West African empires that flourished during the time of the Middle Ages in European

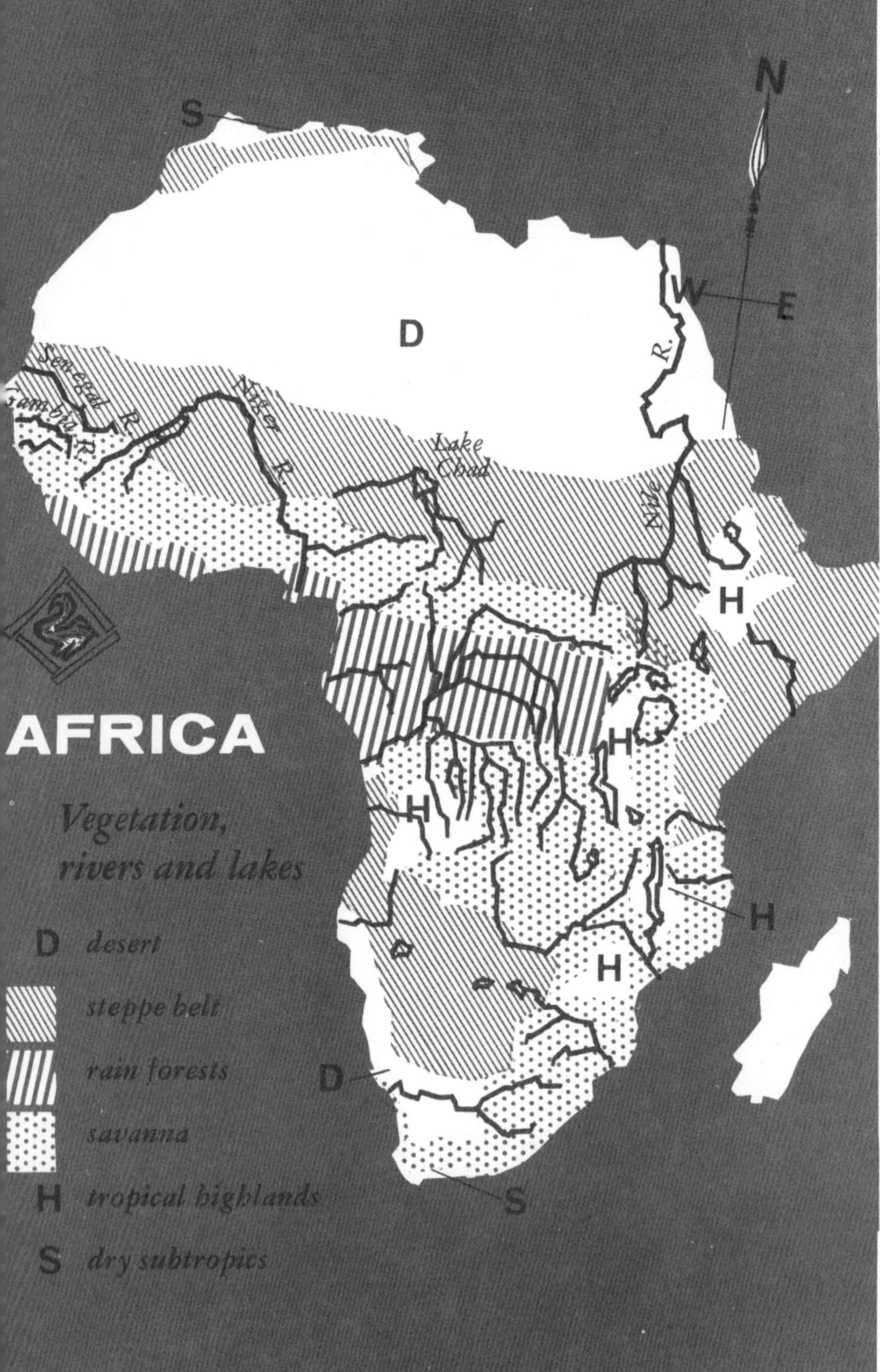
N
W
E
S
D
Sen egal R.
Gambia R.
Niger R.
Lake Chad
Nile R.
H
H
H
H
H
D
S
AFRICA
Vegetation, rivers and lakes
D desert
steppe belt
rain forests
savanna
H tropical highlands
S dry subtropics

history, from about the seventh to the fifteenth centuries. Its fame and influence helped to shape the direction of events not only in Africa but in faraway Europe and Asia as well.

In this volume we will trace briefly the surge of men and events during this early period of Africa's history. For our story we will follow the rise and fall of three powerful ancient kingdoms which dominated the story of West Africa throughout this time. Their names were the kingdoms of *Ghana, Mali,* and *Songhay.* (Remember that Ghana and Mali, as used here, do not refer to the modern nations of West Africa that use these names today.)

Africa is a huge continent, almost three times the area of the continental United States. Africa is a continent of great variety and contrasts. Unless we mark our trails clearly, it will be easy to become lost or confused in our journey in Africa's past. We will consider only that part of Africa north of the equator, roughly the northern half of the continent from the equator to the coast of the Mediterranean Sea.

This huge territory can be divided into four geographical "belts," one on top of another, each sweeping in an east-west direction. Starting from the top down, that is, working from the north (the Mediterranean coast) toward the south (the equator), there is first a narrow coastal temperate zone of fertile soil and relatively mild climate. Today, this area forms the northern parts of Morocco, Algeria, and Tunisia.

Just south of the temperate coastal zone is the world's largest desert, the famed Sahara (the name Sahara means "desert" or "wasteland"). Stretching from the Atlantic coast to the Arabian peninsula, this region of sand dunes and rock piles is an area of very little rainfall. Here and there in the Sahara, there are scattered oases, clumps of trees and vegetation fed by underground wells. For the most part, though, the Sahara consists of 3,500,000 square miles of harsh, bleak wasteland.

Below the Sahara is the savanna land, another belt which stretches across the continent from the Atlantic to the Red Sea. The savanna is an area of tall grass and scattered trees. It is an area of fertile soil and long rainy seasons and short dry seasons. The savanna has sometimes been compared to the prairies of the United States Midwest, which are flat and without mountains or forests.

South of the savanna, along the coastal regions near the equator, are the rain forests. Here, the trees and grasses are so tall and so thick that in many places the sunlight cannot penetrate.

Even with the difficulties of crossing the Sahara and the great forests, the history of this region is a story of mass movements of people. Recent archaeological finds are now shedding new light on the origin of man in Africa (including a suggestion that Africa may have been the cradleland of modern mankind), but the beginning of human beings in Africa remains a mystery.

The people of Africa might be divided into two groups, people of Negroid stock and those of non-Negroid stock. The inhabitants of those regions north of the Sahara are mostly non-Negroids, and Negroids come from south of the Sahara.

A non-Negroid people, known to us today as Berbers, are believed to have been the first people to set up some sort of housekeeping in the Mediterranean coastal region. The area of the Berber states near the Mediterranean came to be known as the Barbary coast.

Many of the Berbers were nomads who moved around constantly in search of grazing lands for their sheep, goats, and horses. The Berber nomads of the desert are called *Tuaregs* (twah-regs). Among the Tuaregs the men often covered their faces with veils, and they became known as the "veiled people." Fierce desert warriors, the Tuaregs sometimes attacked desert travelers and sometimes aided them—it all seemed to depend on the mood and the need of the Tuaregs at the moment.

The vast emptiness of the Sahara made life difficult for people there. Yet, people have always managed somehow to survive in and travel across this region. Desert travel became easier when the one-humped dromedary camel was introduced to the Sahara from Asia, an event that may have taken place when the Romans ruled much of North Africa in the centuries before and after the birth of Christ.

Then as now, camels were unfriendly, nasty-tempered beasts. But their ability to go for long periods without food or water made them good for desert travel. As the use of camels for transporting people and goods became common, caravan routes were established. These, in turn, would develop into important channels of trade and culture which would play key roles in shaping the history of West and North Africa.

Berbers and Tuaregs of the Sahara often came in contact with Negro nomads who also wandered in the great desert. But the center of Negro society was south of the Sahara. Some of the most highly-organized Negro kingdoms developed in the grassland savanna belt. This area came to be known as the Sudan, which means "country of the black people."

A fertile region wedged between the desert on the north and the rain forest on the south, the Sudan is watered by numerous river systems. In the western Sudan, the two most important rivers are the Senegal River and the Niger River.

The Senegal flows westward to empty into the Atlantic Ocean. The Niger, however, takes a roundabout way to flow down to the sea.

From its headwaters near the southwestern corner of Africa's western "hump," the Niger starts inland in a northeasterly direction. After about eight hundred miles the Niger seems to change its mind, making a grand sweeping curve toward the southeast to the Gulf of Guinea. The region where the Niger changes direction is known as the Great Bend.

The early Negro civilizations which developed in the western Sudan were mainly groups of farmers who lived in villages scattered throughout the savannas. The people here worked in the fields near their villages, growing enough food for their own needs and a little left over for trade with other villages.

The inhabitants of the villages were members of several large families, each headed by the oldest male member. The families in any one village were often related to one another by descent from common ancestors, or so they believed. Often, strong links were established between one village and another through intermarriage and trade.

Scattered among the villages were larger towns and cities, often located along important river and trade routes. Some of the towns had populations numbering in the thousands. These people had originally come from the villages, seeking the excitement of urban living and greater opportunities for earning a living.

The towns and cities depended on the villages for food. The people of the towns concentrated instead on crafts, such as weaving cloth, making jewelry, or producing household tools. The biggest business was trade. Many of the larger cities became the great marketplace of the Sudan.

In addition to villagers and townspeople, there were small groups of fishermen and boatmen who settled along the rivers, exchanging fish and transportation services for their food or clothes. Their boats were called pirogues, dugout canoes hewed from a single tree trunk. Along with these river people were other small groups who depended on hunting wild game for their living.

Sudanese families tended to be large. A family included the husband, wife (or often, wives), children, and servants. Sometimes two or three generations might live together in a group of houses. Married sons brought their families to live near their parents and grandparents. To a youngster in such a family, all adult men were "fathers," and all adult women were "mothers," while all the children were "sisters" and "brothers."

Living with the families were servants, either slaves or freemen. (The slaves were usually war captives.) In addition the family might have its own artisans and musician-historians who sang, danced, and acted out the family's history. Sudanese families tended to count wealth not only in terms of goods, gold, or money, but also in the number of people living together as a family.

The great families were linked to other great families to produce a larger organization called the clan. A nation included many clans. At first the clan might occupy a whole village. When it grew more powerful it might wage war, capture more slaves, servants, and freemen, and force surrounding villages to pay tributes. The most powerful of these clans came to win the allegiance or tribute from thousands of people over large areas. These clans were called royal or imperial clans. They ruled over empires.

A major part of the organized life of these Sudanese centered on religious observances—dances, prayers, songs, and special rituals. In the traditional religions of the Sudanese, the people believed in a Creator or High God who caused all things. They also believed that the universe was inhabited by hundreds of lesser gods and spirits. Finally they believed that mysterious magic powers from the Creator God could be used by spirits and men for good or evil.

Religious specialists were the priest-magicians, who asked the gods and spirits to help the people, the crops, and to defend their villages against enemies. Great kings and rulers were thought to have special gifts and powers from the gods.

In the seventh century A.D. a new group of invaders swept into North Africa, causing important changes among the people of the Sahara and the Sudan. The invaders were the Arabs. They too had been desert tribesmen, until they were united by a new faith.

That faith was *Islam* (meaning "submission" to the will of Allah, or God) founded by the Prophet Mohammed of Mecca and Medina (two cities on the

Arabian peninsula which became the holiest cities of Islam). The sacred teachings of Mohammed were preserved in the *Koran,* the holy book of Islam.

Followers of Mohammed (called Moslems, or "ones who submit") were determined to convert nonbelieving "infidels" to the ways of Islam, by force if necessary. Excited by their new faith, the desert cavalry of the Moslems stormed out of the Arabian peninsula. Victories followed victories. Within a hundred years after Mohammed's death (traditionally A.D. 632), the world of Islam stretched eastward to India and westward to the Atlantic coast of North Africa.

Northwest Africa was known to the Arabs as the *Maghreb* (mah-greb). From here the Arabs, joined by Berber converts to Islam, invaded Christian Europe. They conquered most of what is now Spain and Portugal and even a part of southwestern France. Europeans referred to the invaders as Moors, or people from Morocco.

Arab forces had less success in trying to conquer the land of the Sudanese Negroes south of the Sahara. But where Arab arms failed, the teachings of Islam succeeded in crossing the desert. From about A.D. 1000 onward, the Moslem faith gradually assumed greater importance in the western Sudan. For along with this new faith came the Arabic language and the traditions of Moslem scholarship.

In a period when Europe was going through a so-called "dark ages," it was Moslem culture which provided the main advancement of human knowledge. The arts, philosophy, mathematics, and the science of medicine flourished in many parts of the Moslem or the Moslem-influenced world.

Some of the most famous and highly-respected universities in all of the Moslem world were established in the important towns of the western Sudan: Timbuktu, Jenne, Gao. For hundreds of years, these Sudanese cities contributed to the growth of Moslem scholarship and scientific interests. Along with their commercial success, their reputation of wealth and power spread far beyond the western Sudan and their fame lingered long after their golden age had passed.

Against this background, then, we will begin our journey into the history of the western Sudan, visiting in turn the ancient kingdoms of Ghana, Mali, and Songhay.

CHAPTER 1 GHANA
The Land of Gold

The thumping of the royal drums announced the beginning of the ceremonies. Loyal subjects of the kingdom who had business with the king crowded into the great court of the palace. Some fell on their knees and threw dust on their heads, while others clapped their hands, as signs of respect for him. Everyone gazed upon the mighty king. He was dressed in silk, covered with jewels, and wore a cap speckled with gold. Behind his throne stood ten youthful attendants holding shields and armed with swords that had gold handles. Around his pavilion, or tent, were horses outfitted in golden equipment, and hounds "of an excellent breed" wearing gold and silver collars.

To the king's right, the sons of the princes of the empire took their positions. They wore golden ornaments in their hair which added to the glitter of the occasion. The governor of the royal capital and other officials of the empire took their places around the throne.

In the midst of this magnificent display the king conducted the daily affairs of his mighty empire. There were official appointments to be made, and disputes to be settled. There were reports on the condition of the royal treasury to be heard. The king conducted each royal audience in a noble manner which reflected his powerful position as absolute ruler.

Such was the glamour and splendor of the first great empire in West Africa, a wealthy and mighty Negro empire that came to be known as Ghana. In its own time the fame and glory of Ghana spread far beyond its own borders.

The King of Ghana conducting the daily affairs of his mighty empire.

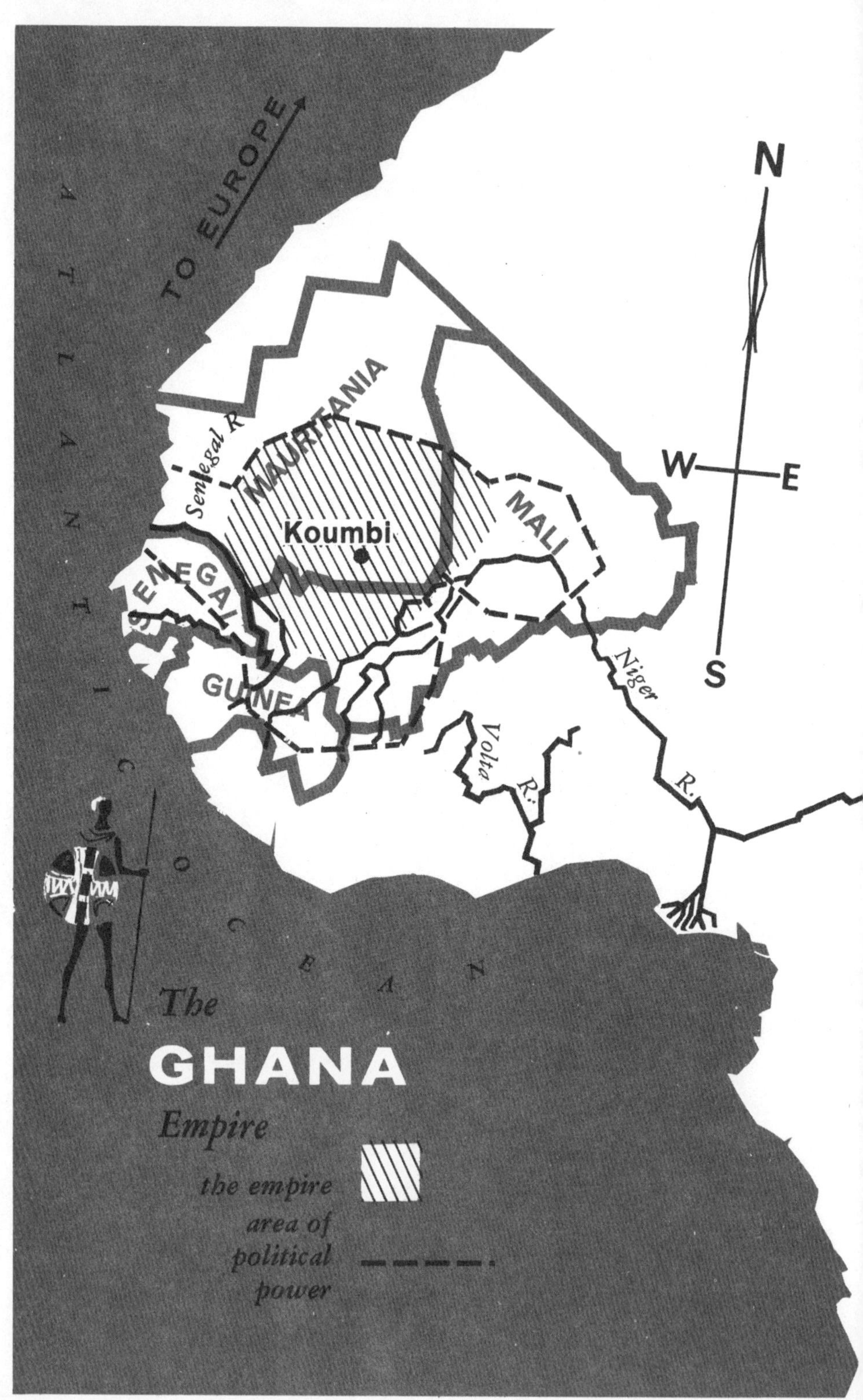

TO EUROPE
N
W
E
S
MAURITANIA
Senegal R.
Koumbi
MALI
SENEGAL
GUINEA
Niger
R.
Volta
R.
ATLANTIC OCEAN
The
GHANA
Empire
the empire
area of
political
power

LOCATION AND ORIGIN OF GHANA

The earliest days of Ghana was a time long before modern surveying techniques were developed. At that time, no one thought it necessary to stake out territorial claims with well-defined boundaries. For this reason we today do not know the exact boundaries of the old Ghanaian Empire. Perhaps no one ever knew the exact points at which Ghanaian territory began and left off.

Scholars have established, however, that the heartland of the Ghanaian Empire was set in a region of the western Sudan, northeast of the Senegal River and northwest of the Niger River. At the height of its power, Ghana controlled territories westward across the Senegal River to the Atlantic Ocean, southward to a point approaching the headwaters of the Niger River, and eastward to the region where the mighty Niger makes its "great southern bend." On its northern side the Ghanaian Empire edged into the trackless wastelands of the Sahara.

If someone were to draw a rough outline of the Ghanaian Empire onto a map of Africa as it looks today, the outer reaches of the old empire would include parts of several present-day African nations—Mauritania, Mali, Senegal, and Guinea.

Many different peoples have lived in this region between the Senegal and Niger Rivers. They were there long before the history of the region was recorded. Among the first of the groups to hold great political power were a people known as the *Soninkes* (son-in-kays).

The Soninke people were actually a group of related tribes. Each tribe in turn was composed of several clans

—a group of families descended from one ancestor. Among the Soninkes there were clans that bore names like *Sisse* (see-say), *Drame* (dra-may), *Kante* (kan-tay), *Sylla* (sil-la), and others. Curiously enough the division of labor in the kingdom often seemed to correspond to the division of tribes and clans.

The Sisse family, for example, was the ruling clan among the Soninkes. It provided the kings and most of the officials and heads of the provinces. The Kante clan specialized in metalworking and provided the blacksmiths. Other clans might be engaged in such work as farming, fishing, clothmaking, or cattle breeding.

All of the Soninke people spoke a language called *Mande* (man-day), although the Soninkes were not the only Mande speakers in the region. Other groups also used this language. Mande-speaking people are found today in many parts of West Africa.

According to Soninke traditions passed down by word of mouth from one generation to the next, the beginning of the Ghanaian Empire dates back to about the year A.D. 300. Its start was not exactly encouraging. At about that time conquerors drifted into the area from the north and seized control of the land. These invaders were probably people of Berber origin, migrating from North Africa. The Berbers were wandering nomad tribes from the northern edge of the Sahara Desert. They stayed for a long time—possibly as long as five hundred years. A Berber ruling dynasty was set up and remained in power until about A.D. 700.

"Local rule" returned to the Soninke people when a warrior from the Sisse clan executed a successful revolt against the Berber dynasty. Under Soninke leadership Ghana embarked on a fabulous period of development and expansion. Two metals played key roles in the growth of the empire—iron which was used for the weapons, and gold which made the empire rich.

ULTIMATE WEAPONS OF ANCIENT DAYS

No one knows for sure when or how the craft of ironworking came about in the western Sudan. Some scientists have found evidence in the village of Nok (in what is now northern Nigeria) which indicates that iron may have been mined and worked in West Africa at the time of Christ. Knowledge of iron was to bring great changes for the people of West Africa, as it did for their societies.

Iron ore was—and still is—plentiful in many parts of West Africa. It was easier to obtain than some of the metals used earlier, such as copper or bronze. Tools made of iron were harder and more useful than copper, bronze, stone, bone, or wooden ones. By using iron tools, farming reached new levels of productivity in West Africa.

Even more significant, perhaps, was the role of iron as the "ultimate weapon" of its day. People who had weapons made of iron could defeat those who did not. The people who had iron often demonstrated this advantage through conquests. These conquests brought many political and social changes. As the strong group conquered its weaker neighbors, many individual groups were joined into a single, much larger, and more developed society. Ghana built its empire in just this manner.

The Soninke-ruled people of Ghana were apparently the first—and for a long time, the only—users of iron in their region of Africa. The people of the empire of Ghana attacked and defeated their neighbors sometime before A.D. 300.

These neighbors of the Ghanaians did not have iron and they fought with bars of ebony, a dark hard wood. An Arab historian of that time has noted that the Ghanaians "can defeat them because they (the Ghanaians) fight with swords and lances." No doubt, the swords and lances of the Ghanaians were made of iron.

Sometimes the conquered regions became part of Ghana itself and were placed under the direct control of the Ghanaian king. At other times the defeated local ruler was permitted to remain in power in his own land, so long as he pledged his allegiance to Ghana. Ghana's king retained the right to appoint governors in the important cities and towns. And each of the states that came under his power had the "privilege" of contributing to the Ghanaian treasury. Also every tribe and clan was expected to contribute fighting men for the combined army of the empire.

Among the regions that came under Ghanaian control or influence were areas on the Upper Senegal (say-naygal) and Upper Niger regions. As we shall see later, the empires of Mali and Songhay (song-gay) were founded here.

ISLAM REACHES GHANA

Until A.D. 700, Ghana remained a shadowy kingdom. It had no written history, for the Soninkes and the Berbers in that area had not devised a system of writing.

Though a lively trade had long since developed between the Negro kingdom (Ghana) in the Sudan (the

Trade Routes of the

GHANA

Empire

salt mines

gold fields

TO EUROPE

ATLANTIC OCEAN

Sidjilmassa

Taghaza

Tadmekka

Aoudaghasi

Koumbi

Gao

Sia

Senegal R.

Gambia

BAMBUK

BURE

Niger R.

Volta R.

N

W

E

name of the region in which Ghana was located) and the commercial centers of Northwest Africa, and though camel caravans were plodding their way across the Sahara to and from Ghana on a fairly regular basis, Ghana and its fabulous wealth remained virtually unknown to the world outside of West and Northwest Africa.

By A.D. 681, Arab conquerors from the Middle East had swept all the way across North Africa and had arrived at Africa's western coast. The Arab advance halted only temporarily at the water's edge. Across the narrow Strait of Gibraltar lay Spain and the rest of Christian Europe. Arab warriors were not going to let a narrow strip of water stop them for long.

From the conquered people of Morocco, called Moors, the Arabs first heard of another prize worthy of their attention—a Negro kingdom south of the Sahara which had a seemingly inexhaustible supply of gold. The Arabs were definitely interested in getting a first-hand look for themselves.

So they split their forces into two columns. One of them, the northern force, crossed the Strait of Gibraltar at about A.D. 712 to invade Spain. The other column was to strike southward, following the caravan routes across the Sahara to seek the source of Sudanese gold.

For the Arabs and the Moorish converts to Islam, the invasion of Spain proceeded splendidly. The forces of Islam spilled into much of the Iberian peninsula and penetrated across the Pyrénées mountains into what is now southern France before they were halted at the Battle of Tours in A.D. 732.

At just about this time the southern invasion column started on its way toward Ghana. Though the Arab forces seemed almost irresistible in the northern invasion, their southern expedition had little success. In fact the invasion of Ghana turned out to be a flop.

To the surprise of the desert warriors, their attack was repelled by a powerful Ghanaian army. Many of the Arabs in the invasion force promptly thought better of the whole thing. They gave up the idea of conquest, settled down in western Saharan and Sudanese towns, and joined the Berbers in becoming traders.

If the Arabs had failed in their attempt to control the western Sudan, they had at least established direct contact between the Moslem and the Negro worlds. This contact was to benefit both worlds. From this time on, trans-Saharan caravan trade flourished and multiplied—gold and slaves moving from the south to the north; salt, horses, cloth, swords, books, and other goods transported from the north in return.

With the goods came ideas. The teachings of Islam began to spread throughout West Africa. Moslem learning and scientific interests, and possibly the most important of all, a written Arabic language, came to the western Sudan. Virtually all that we know about the kingdom of Ghana and the other Sudanese states was preserved for us by the Arab and Negro scholars and travelers of that time. The language in which they wrote was Arabic.

HOW GHANA GOT ITS NAME

The Ghanaians themselves called their land the kingdom of *Ouagadou* (wa-ga-doo). How then did it come to be known as the empire of Ghana?

Ghana in Mande, the language of the Soninkes, meant "warrior king" and was one of the titles of the kings of

Ouagadou. Another title that these kings had was *Kaya Magha* (ka-yah ma-gah), or "king of gold," reflecting Ouagadou's vast gold resources. Through most of Ouagadou's period of greatness, the Soninke kings kept their capital at a city called *Koumbi* (koom-bi).

As the fame and wealth of the Soninke warrior kings (the Ghanas) spread into North Africa, people there began to refer to the capital of the Ghanas simply as Ghana. Soon they referred to the entire kingdom as Ghana.

In this way, then, the title of the kings of Ouagadou was extended to include Koumbi, the capital of Ouagadou. Later the name Ghana was extended further to serve as a sort of shorthand for the entire kingdom of Ouagadou.

THE MIGHTY GHANAS

Judging from the surprise shown by the Arab historians of Ghana, the Arabs had not expected to find such a highly-organized Negro society tucked away in the savannas, the grassy plains, of West Africa. At the head of Ghana's political structure was the King of Ouagadou, the patriarch or father of the Soninke people. He was their military chief, their religious leader, the chief of justice, and the supreme overseer of the empire. It was a custom in Ghana that when the king died, he was *not* succeeded by his own son, but by the son of his sister. This system of determining heirs is called the "matrilineal principle of succession" and it is still practiced today in parts of West Africa.

As patriarch it was the duty of the king to settle disputes between his individual subjects and between the various tribes and clans. Justice was pronounced by royal decrees during glittering ceremony, as we have already described earlier.

For those of his subjects who could not attend the grand show at the palace, the king thoughtfully toured his capital city daily, talking to his subjects and listening to their complaints. So much fanfare usually accompanied these kingly tours that hardly any of his subjects could possibly miss his coming.

Ghana's judicial system had both a lower court and a court of appeal. But the king was more or less the supreme court of the land. There was no question as to whether he could make his decisions stick, since the king was also commander-in-chief of one of the biggest armies of the time. This army was not only useful in keeping troublesome neighbors in their places, but was more than adequate to keep the peace within Ghana's own borders.

El-Bekri, an Arab scholar, wrote that the "King of Ghana can put 200,000 warriors in the field, more than 40,000 of them being armed with bow and arrow." The rest presumably were armed with spears. El-Bekri made this notation on the strength of the Ghanaian army in the year 1067, or one year after Duke William of Normandy crossed the English Channel to conquer Anglo-Saxon England.

Historians have wondered what the Normans, who mustered a cross-Channel invasion force of 10,000 to 15,000 knights and soldiers, might have thought of their chances if they were attacking Ghana instead of England. Of course, it is highly doubtful that Duke William and his Normans had ever heard of Ghana. At that time, many Europeans were barely aware of the existence of Africa.

LIFEBLOOD OF EMPIRE

Peace and prosperity prevailed in West Africa in the glorious days of the Ghanaian Empire during the tenth and eleventh centuries. Ghana was a land of rich and fertile fields where millet, sorghum, and cotton were grown. But the Ghanaians themselves were not primarily interested in farming, because the lifeblood of the empire was trade.

Ghana was the great trading center of West Africa. Caravans came from all over Africa to trade for Ghana's gold and salt.

Caravans brought to Ghana all types of goods, including much of the foodstuffs on which the Ghanaians depended for their daily meals. These were traded for locally-produced merchandise, such as cotton cloth, metal ornaments, or leather goods. (The highly-prized Morocco leather did not originate in Morocco, but in the savanna zones of West Africa.) By far the two most important items of trade were gold and salt.

To a large extent Ghana's wealth was based on its control over the gold-producing regions of West Africa. At times so much gold flowed into Ghana that it almost proved to be embarrassing. The gold supply had to be strictly regulated to keep the price from going too low.

The rulers of Ghana were well aware of the need to uphold the value of their chief source of wealth. To do this, they took a portion of the gold supply out of circulation by issuing an order that only the King of Ghana could possess gold in nugget form. Everyone else simply had to get along with gold dust. "Without this precaution," commented El-Bekri approvingly, "gold would become so plentiful (in Ghana) that it would practically lose its value."

Under this rule all gold nuggets were promptly turned over to the King of Ghana. The people obeyed this rule faithfully because the king had them convinced that it was dangerous to own gold nuggets. They were told that all manner of misfortunes would happen to those who possessed nuggets. What about the king himself? Well, he let it be known that he was blessed by protecting spirits so that, for him, owning gold nuggets was perfectly safe.

Indeed, the king's splendid collection of gold nuggets included a single magnificent lump that was said to weigh thirty pounds! (If that does not sound like much, think of it this way. The price of pure gold in the United States is officially listed as $35 per troy ounce, and a thirty-pound lump of gold today would be worth $12,600!)

The King of Ghana used one of his nuggets as a tether or hitching post for his horse. This was perhaps the most expensive hitching post of all time. Little wonder that awed Arab writers described the Ghanaian kings as "the richest in the world because of their gold."

Surprisingly enough, one item that was often worth more, pound for pound, than gold in Ghana, was salt. For salt was as scarce in the western Sudan as gold was plentiful. Salt, of course, is an essential part of human diets. Because of the scarcity of salt in their region, the people of the savanna zone were said to have developed a craving for it.

There was plenty of salt to be had in the northern Sahara. And since the people north of the desert had salt and wanted gold, and the people in the south had gold and wanted salt, the result was a heavy trans-Saharan gold-salt trade.

The trade route started in the north at the commercial city of *Sidjilmassa* (sid-jil-ma-sah) (near today's Moroccan-Algerian frontier), it wound past the salt-rich region near the village of *Taghaza* (ta-ga-zah) (in present-day Algeria), across the desert to Ghana and to the gold-bearing regions south of Ghana.

The kingdom of Ghana had the great good fortune of straddling this lucrative trade route. The movement of gold and salt back and forth across its land made Ghana rich.

THE MYSTERY OF *Wangara* (wang-ga-rah)

The Arab traders who did business with Ghana all knew where its gold came from. It came from a region called Wangara. However, very few people knew where Wangara was. And the people who did know recognized a valuable secret when they saw one. They were not going to tell anybody about Wangara's location and spoil the trade for themselves. This lack of specific knowledge on Wangara did not discourage people from trying to locate it.

A writer-geographer named El-Edrisi (an Arab nobleman in the service of the King of Sicily) described Wangara as an island 300 miles long and 150 miles wide, surrounded by the waters of the Nile River. During part of the year floodwaters submerged this island. But when the water receded, people of nearby regions paddled out to the island to collect the gold washed up by the flood. They stayed there on the job until the flood returned.

More recent historians dispute the contention that Wangara was anywhere near the Nile River. For the early writers on Africa had a tendency to confuse *every* river on the continent with the Nile. The "Nile" mentioned by Edrisi flowed from east to west and was most probably the Senegal River. Indeed, many modern African historians believe that ancient gold fields around the regions of *Bambuk* (bahm-book) and *Bure* (boo-ray), near the Senegal River, may have been the fabled Wangara. The Bambuk-Bure fields were capable of supplying huge quantities of gold for centuries.

The regions of Bambuk and Bure are so laced with rivers—the Senegal, the Niger, and tributaries to both rivers—that portions of dry ground in that region could have been mistaken for islands. Furthermore, some gold is still being worked in those regions, between the rise and fall of floods, just the way Edrisi had described it.

The mystery of Wangara has baffled geographers and historians, as well as explorers and fortune-hunters, down to the present. Other areas beside Bambuk-Bure have laid claim to being the "true Wangara." Among those with supportable claims is the region of Lobi on the Volta River to the southeast. Since gold is found in many areas of West Africa, it is possible that the various regions served as the main source of gold during different periods, and each was the "true Wangara" of its own time.

There was little doubt that the empire of Ghana maintained control over Wangara's gold production during the empire's days of glory. But it is doubtful that even the powerful kings of Ghana maintained effective political control over the people who inhabited the Wangara gold fields. For these people were either shy or unfriendly or both. They were certainly cautious. Despite the heavy traffic of gold traders in the vicinity of Wangara, the visiting merchants rarely saw a Wangara gold miner—and never spoke to one.

The Wangara gold trade was conducted through the curious custom of "dumb barter" or silent trade. In "dumb barter" the trading partners conducted their business without ever seeing or speaking to each other!

The procedure was something like this. Arab traders and their caravans laden with goods and salt would enter Ghana. There they met Ghanaian middlemen, who guided the caravans to specific trading spots on the banks of the rivers in the gold country.

On arriving at the trading site the merchants would beat large drums to signal the opening of the market. The traders piled the goods and salt in rows, each merchant identifying his own piles with special marks. Then the caravan would pull back a half day's journey from the trading site.

While the caravan was gone, the Negro gold miners of Wangara arrived in boats, and brought their gold. They would heap a quantity of gold beside each pile of goods and salt that the merchants had left behind. Then they too retired from the scene.

Once more the merchants came back to the site of the trading. If they found that the miners had left a satisfactory quantity of gold for their goods, they picked up the gold and went their way, beating on their drums to show that their business was concluded.

But if the traders decided that the Wangara miners had not left enough gold to pay for the salt and other stuff, they would leave the piles untouched, hoping that the miners would return and add to their gold offerings. This went on until a bargain, satisfactory to both sides, was struck.

Finally each group returned to the trading site separately to collect the goods they had obtained in the exchange, going their separate ways once again, satisfied and happy.

In this silent trade (it was silent if one can disregard all of the drum beating) the exact locations of the Wangara gold fields were never revealed. According to one tale, several gold merchants once ambushed and captured a Wangara gold miner and tried to force him to tell all about Wangara's gold. The miner went to his death without uttering a word. This treacherous act so angered the people of Wangara that three years passed before they would resume the gold trade. And they resumed it only because they had no other way to satisfy their desperate need for salt.

THE SOURCE OF THE SALT

Though the source of Wangara's gold remained a well-kept secret, the source of the salt in the trans-

Saharan trade was no secret at all. Practically all of it came from the great salt mines at the town of Taghaza in the middle of the desert country.

Aside from a lot of salt, though, Taghaza didn't seem to have very much of anything else. But salt alone was enough to make Taghaza important. For such was the need for salt in the western Sudan (which had none of its own) that salt was the one item for which the miners of Wangara were always willing to exchange their gold. The trans-Saharan gold trade might never have amounted to much had it not been for the salt mines of Taghaza.

The best descriptions of Taghaza that we have today were written well after the Ghanaian Empire had disintegrated. So far as we can tell, Taghaza had no startling political history until the sixteenth century, despite its importance to the gold-salt trade for centuries earlier.

In the middle of the fourteenth century a famous Arab traveler named *Ibn Battuta* (ib-bin ba-tu-tah) passed through Taghaza. He described Taghaza as "an unattractive village, with the curious feature that its houses and mosques (Moslem temples) are built of blocks of salt, roofed with camel skins. There are no trees there, nothing but sand. In the sand is a salt mine; they dig for the salt, and find it in thick slabs. . . ."

Conditions in Taghaza were so desolate and miserable that the slaves who worked in the salt mines were the only permanent residents. Taghaza was hometown to them simply because they, being slaves, had no choice in the matter.

The climate and soil conditions around Taghaza were not the least bit suited for farming. No food could be

Ibn Battuta recorded much of what we know today about the history of the western Sudan.

grown locally. The inhabitants of Taghaza depended on the caravans to bring them their food. They survived on millet (which was brought all the way from the western Sudan across the desert), on camel steaks, and on dates brought from a region known as Drar and from Sidjilmassa in Morocco. Both of these places were about twenty days away, as the caravans traveled. Often, during long intervals between caravan visits, some of the slaves would die for lack of food.

Water too was in critically short supply. The inhabitants of Taghaza were forced to drink water drawn from wells near the salt pits. This water tasted like liquefied salt.

In spite of the ghastly working and living conditions in Taghaza, Ibn Battuta reported that the business done at Taghaza amounted to an enormous figure in terms of hundredweights of gold dust. "The Negroes use salt as a medium of exchange, just as gold and silver are used (elsewhere); they cut it up (the slabs of salt) into pieces and buy and sell with it."

Down through the sixteenth century Taghaza's salt mines were still being worked by slaves. And caravans starting at the commercial city of Sidjilmassa were still stopping at Taghaza to pick up a supply of salt to carry across the Sahara to the western Sudan, where the salt could be exchanged for Wangara's gold.

KOUMBI—AT THE CROSSROADS OF TRADE

As we have noted, the Ghanaian Empire could not exert complete control over the timid, mysterious gold miners of Wangara. And the boundaries of Ghana never extended far enough north to include the salt mines at Taghaza. Yet Ghana completely dominated the gold-salt trade. This was because the merchant caravans could not get from Taghaza to Wangara and back again without crossing the territory of Ghana.

Sitting in the path of the caravan routes was the Ghanaian capital, the city of Koumbi. This city became the busiest marketplace of its time in West Africa. Gold and salt were the most important—but by no means the only—items offered in trade.

To the markets of Koumbi, Arab and Negro merchants brought a seemingly endless variety of goods for sale. There were cattle, sheep, and honey brought from the south; wheat from North Africa; raisins, dried fruits, and other foodstuffs from all over. There was cloth called *chigguyiya* (cheeg-goo-yee-yah) for sale, along with red and blue blouses imported all the way from Spain, robes from Morocco, locally made leather goods, and tassels of pure gold thread. Gum arabic was sold to merchants who exported it to Spain, where it was used in the preparation of silk. There were cowries (seashells used as currency in certain regions), copper, ivory, pearls, and of course lots and lots of gold and salt. Gold dust was the usual medium of exchange for buying and selling in the great Koumbi market.

The shops of the local craftsmen dotted the marketplaces. Ghanaian ironsmiths made weapons for the king's army. Gold and coppersmiths made jewelry for the king as well as for the general trade. There were clothweavers, potters, sandalmakers—and there were the slave traders.

Slavery was commonly practiced at that time in all parts of the Sudan, from one side of the African continent to the other. Koumbi had one of the largest slave markets in the region. Its market was kept supplied by steady raiding of weaker groups who lived on the southern frontiers of the Ghanaian Empire.

Slaving was a profitable—though ugly—business. Merchants from North Africa would risk long and difficult journeys across the Sahara to buy Sudanese slaves. They knew that there was always a ready market for human slaves in the north.

Ghana had many expert craftsmen who made weapons from iron. They also made jewelry from gold and copper.

The King of Ghana received a handsome income from the trade of his empire. This income came from the power of the Ghanaian rulers to collect taxes from the merchants. Each merchant, for example, had to pay one dinar of gold in taxes before he could bring one donkey-load of salt into Koumbi. He had to pay *another* two dinars in gold for the privilege of taking that same donkey-load of salt out of Koumbi.

In other words, every time a donkey-load of salt passed through town, the Ghanaian ruler in Koumbi was three dinars richer. (A dinar, by the way, was defined as the weight of 72 grains of barley.)

Other goods brought to or passing through Ghana were also taxed. El-Bekri reported that the going tax rate on every camel- or donkey-load of copper was about five eighths of an ounce of gold. General merchandise was taxed at the rate of one ounce of gold per load. These tariffs (taxes on imports and exports), plus the tributes from vassal kingdoms and the gold nuggets turned over to the king, helped to keep the Ghanaian royal treasury in excellent financial condition.

Even if complaining might help, the merchants were not likely to gripe too much. The taxes were small enough so that they did not cut too deeply into the merchants' profits. Moreover, the money collected helped to pay for Ghana's elaborate government, which maintained peace and order throughout the kingdom. Commerce prospered under these conditions. And though the merchants were not exactly eager to pay their taxes, they certainly got their money's worth from the efficiency and security provided by the Ghanaian government.

THE "TWIN CITIES"

According to the accounts of Arab writers, the capital of Ghana was actually composed of "twin cities." Koumbi was divided into two separate towns linked by a long avenue. The centers of these two towns were some six to ten miles apart.

The land between the two towns was dotted with houses so that it was not always possible to tell where one town stopped and the other one began. This situation was somewhat similar to that found in many of our own large metropolitan areas, where the suburban towns tend to run into each other.

One of Koumbi's two towns served as the commercial center of the empire. This town was inhabited almost entirely by Arab and Berber merchants. Since these merchants were Moslems, this town had no less than a dozen mosques. Each of these mosques had its own Moslem ministers—the Imam—and full-time readers of the *Koran* (Islam's holy book).

The Arabs called the second of Koumbi's two towns *El-Ghaba* (el-ga-bah), meaning "The Forest." Within the limits of El-Ghaba was a grove of prickly bushes and thorns. This grove, or "forest," was sacred to the Negroes of Ghana.

El-Ghaba was not only the spiritual but also the royal capital of the empire of Ghana. Encircled by a protecting stone wall, El-Ghaba had a single mosque for the use of visiting Moslem dignitaries. Most of the houses in El-Ghaba were built of wood or clay, with straw roofing. The wealthy and important residents lived in homes made of wood and stone. The most impressive building in town, of course, was the king's palace.

The royal palace was said to be "a fortress and several huts with rounded roofs, all being enclosed by a wall." But the palace of the king was not the usual dark, drafty kind of castle. Several windows allowed plenty of light inside. And its chambers and halls were decorated with sculpture and paintings, reflecting a well-developed royal taste in art. In the palace at El-Ghaba the King of Ghana held court with all the glamour and splendor that his considerable wealth and power could muster.

Aside from his privilege of living in a palace and the right to collect gold nuggets, the king enjoyed other special benefits. El-Bekri reported that among the non-Moslem residents of Koumbi, only the king and his heir were permitted to wear clothes that were sewn. All the other non-Moslems wore lengths of cotton, silk, or brocade cloths which they draped around themselves.

During the later years of the Ghanaian Empire, the dress code was relaxed a bit. By that time each citizen was allowed to dress according to what he could afford.

The empire of Ghana had several different capitals during the many centuries of its existence. But Koumbi was the capital of Ghana when the empire was at the height of its glory. In a later period, Koumbi was repeatedly attacked and sacked. In time, it disappeared altogether and became a "lost city" of history.

It was not until the twentieth century that archaeologists went back in search of the lost Koumbi. Near a region now known as *Koumbi Saleh* (koom-bi sa-lay), scientists dug into the soil and uncovered the ruins of a large town. This town covered a square mile and might have supported thirty thousand people. And ten miles away from there, scientists uncovered the ruins of a second town. This site was known to the local people there as Ghanata.

We may never be sure whether Koumbi Saleh is the Koumbi of the Ghanaian Empire, or if Ghanata is El-Ghaba. The similarity of names may or may not mean anything. In that region there are many places now which have Koumbi as part of their names.

Among the many objects recovered at the Koumbi Saleh excavation site were iron lances, knives, nails, farming tools, fragments of pottery, glass weights for measuring gold, painted stone bearing verses from the Koran in Arabic script, and one of the finest pairs of scissors of that era ever to be found in any part of the world.

Because of what they found, scientists strongly suspect that Koumbi Saleh and Ghanata are indeed the "twin cities" that once were the capital of the Ghanaian Empire.

THE LEGEND OF *Ouagadou-Bida* (wa-ga-doo-bee-dah)

As the trade of the western Sudan increased, more and more Moslem Arab and Berber merchants came to Ghana to stay. The Islamic faith was freely practiced in Ghana. Many of the Moslems, because of their learning and their skill in commerce, were chosen to serve as ministers to the King of Ghana.

Because of the strong missionary efforts of the Moslems, many of the people in the Ghanaian Empire were converted to the faith of Islam. Among the ruling Soninke group, however, only a relatively few chose the Moslem religion. Most of the Soninkes clung to their own traditional beliefs—the worship of Ouagadou-Bida.

Soninke traditions tell us that Ouagadou-Bida was a great snake that lived in a dark cave in the Sacred Grove of Ghana's royal capital. This holy serpent was the protecting spirit of the Sisse clan (part of the Soninke people) of the Ghanaian rulers. Since the king was the protector of the empire, Ouagadou-Bida became the protecting spirit of the entire kingdom. This is why the Ghanaians called their land the kingdom of Ouagadou.

The Sacred Grove was located a short distance from the royal palace. The grove was probably a thicket of thorny shrubs. Whether a great snake actually lived in this grove was not really important. The important thing was that, to the pagans of Ghana, the Sacred Grove was the most important place in the spiritual life of their nation (like the Holy Land in the Christian religion). Priests of Ouagadou-Bida jealously guarded the Sacred Grove to make sure that nonbelievers and intruders were kept out.

The King of Ghana entered the Sacred Grove only once during his lifetime. His one-time visit came on the occasion of his elevation to the throne, when the priests of Ouagadou-Bida made sacrifices to the serpent spirit for the new monarch.

The Sacred Grove also held the royal tombs. When the king died, his body was returned to the grove for burial. To make sure that the dead king would not be in want in the next world, food, drink, robes, and his personal ornaments such as weapons, carpets, cushions,

According to legend, the empire of Ghana declined because the brave warrior Amadou killed the snake spirit Ouagadou-Bida.

and mats were buried with him. Unhappily for some of the palace servants, their jobs did not end with the king's death. They too were sealed in the tomb to continue serving their master in the afterlife.

In Soninke tradition, there was an Ouagadou-Bida legend which traced the rise and fall of the Ghanaian Empire. According to this legend, the worship of Ouagadou-Bida required an annual human sacrifice. Each year the most beautiful girl of Koumbi was sacrificed in the Sacred Grove to appease the serpent deity.

One year, so the legend went, the priests of Ghana chose to sacrifice a beautiful girl named *Sia* (see-ah). The lovely Sia, it turned out, was engaged to be married to a mighty warrior named *Amadou Sefedokote* (Ah-ma-doo say-fay-do-ko-tay) (whose name meant "Amadou Who Says Little").

Not surprisingly, Amadou was most upset by the outcome of Koumbi's annual beauty contest. On the day of the sacrifice he crept into the Sacred Grove and hid behind a tree. When the serpent spirit came out of the cave, Amadou leaped forward and sliced off its head with his sword.

Ouagadou-Bida was no ordinary serpent. It promptly grew a new head to replace the one that had been severed, or cut off. Fortunately Amadou was not only strong and silent, he had a lot of fight in him. He hacked off the serpent's heads just as fast as the spirit could replace them. The serpent's severed heads whistled through the air and landed in regions such as Bambuk and Bure, which immediately became gold-bearing regions.

Finally, after Amadou had cut off the seventh head, Ouagadou-Bida collapsed and died. Amadou mounted a great white steed (a horse with tremendous spirit), snatched up Sia, and galloped off while all the people of Koumbi cursed him and wept.

The people of Koumbi knew that without their protective spirit, Ouagadou-Bida, the kingdom of Ghana was doomed. Sure enough, a terrible period of drought followed. Grains would not grow in the fields. Flocks of animals died from thirst. Terror-stricken, the Soninkes took flight. They became nomads, wandering from place to place, always cherishing the memory of a once-great empire which died with Ouagadou-Bida.

Such was the end of the Ghanaian Empire, according to legend. History tells a somewhat different story. The historical version of Ghana's end was not as fanciful, but no less tragic than the legend.

THE *Almoravids* (al-mo-ra-vids)

From the eighth century on, the influence of Ghana in West Africa increased, until the empire reached the height of its powers in the mid-eleventh century. The high point of Ghanaian history came in the 1060s. Just one decade (ten years) after Ghana reached its height, it plunged into a headlong decline from which it never recovered.

For years Ghana's wealth had been an object of jealousy among its neighbors. Enemies of Ghana frequently raided the regions on the fringes of the empire. Only an efficient government and a powerful army enabled the kings of Ghana to keep the empire together through the first half of the eleventh century (1000–1050). But at that time a powerful new force swept through West

Africa. A Moslem preacher named *Ibn Yacin* (ib-bin ya-seen) founded his Almoravid sect, a reform group of Moslems. Ibn Yacin's reputation attracted many followers. Desert tribes rallied to his banners. The Almoravids unleashed a wave of religious feeling which soon made Ibn Yacin the master of the western Sahara.

The overthrow of the Negro kingdom of Ghana was a cherished ambition among the Almoravids. Though

Abu Bakr was the leader of the Almoravids who invaded Ghana and destroyed Koumbi. This invasion led to the decline of Ghana as the most powerful empire in West Africa.

many Moslems lived in Ghana, worked there, and even served the Ghanaian king, the empire of Ghana was basically a pagan state. Most of its people continued to worship Ouagadou-Bida. Still, the pagan rulers of Ghana treated the Moslem population fairly and in a friendly way. The Almoravids, however, did not return the Ghanaian's religious freedom in kind.

After Ibn Yacin's death in 1057, a follower named

Abu Bakr assumed leadership of the Almoravid forces in the southern Sahara. In 1062 he was ready to invade the Ghanaian Empire. By 1067 the fanatical Almoravid warriors were hammering at the gates of Koumbi itself.

Under King *Bassi* (ba-see) and his successor, King *Tenka Menin* (ten-ka men-in), the Ghanaians resisted heroically for almost a decade. But in 1076 or 1077, Koumbi fell to the Almoravids. The city was destroyed. The Almoravids slew many of the citizens and seized their property.

The desert conquerors forced the Ghanaians to pay tribute and taxes, and to accept the Moslem religion. Those who resisted were massacred.

END OF AN OLD EMPIRE, BEGINNING OF A NEW

The ranks of the Almoravids were made up of fierce desert tribesmen. These tribes remained united so long as they had a common cause and a common enemy. But once they accomplished their goal, they usually fell to fighting among themselves.

On the death of Abu Bakr in 1087, Almoravid power south of the Sahara simply fell apart. The Almoravids' stay in Ghana had been relatively short, but it proved disastrous for Ghana. When the Soninke rulers tried to re-establish their control over the Ghanaian Empire, they ran into many problems.

Many of their former states had broken away from Koumbi's domination. The kingdoms of Songhay, Mandingo, and Tekrur were among those who declared their independence. Some of these groups had been converted to Islam, and they weren't interested in rejoining a pagan Soninke kingdom.

TO EUROPE

ALMORAVIDS ROUTE

N
W
E
S

Aoudaghasi
Walata
Timbuktu
Koumbi
TEKRUR
Sosso
Niger
SONGHAY
Niger R.
Gambia R.
MANDINGO
Volta R.

ATLANTIC OCEAN

Decline of the GHANA Empire

independent of Koumbi rule

Sosso drive in 1203

During the twelfth century the once-proud Ghanaian Empire decayed and disintegrated. Individual groups fought constantly with one another. Finally, in 1180, the southern branch of the Soninkes established a rival kingdom around the city of *Sosso* (so-so). The pagan kings of Sosso tried once more to re-create the Ghanaian Empire.

The most powerful of the Sosso kings was *Sumanguru* (su-man-gu-ru), a member of the Kante clan. Sumanguru brought his army to Koumbi and conquered it in 1203. Like previous conquerors, Sumanguru demanded heavy taxes from the residents of the city.

Sumanguru's Sosso kingdom did not last long. In 1235 the army of the Sossos was defeated by the forces of a rising new power in the western Sudan, a Mandingo kingdom called Mali. Five years later the victorious Malians conquered and sacked Koumbi for the last time. Ghana, a once-great empire, vanished.

CHAPTER 2 MALI
Empire of the Mandingoes

The furious invasion by the Moslem Almoravids had shattered the empire of Ghana beyond repair. But as this empire faced its death, another was in the process of being born.

As the power of Ghana decreased, many of its states claimed their independence. Among these was a Mandingo state, the kingdom of Mali. Before the thirteenth century, Mali was unimportant. The capital of Mali was a city called *Kangaba* (kan-ga-bah), on the Niger River, about 250 miles south of Koumbi. The Mandingo people of Mali were distantly related to the Soninkes and the Sossos. Actually all of them represented various tribal branches of the same family group. They all spoke the Mande language.

In one way, though, the Mandingoes differed from the Soninkes and Sossos. The Soninkes clung to their traditional gods until the Almoravids forced them to accept the Islamic faith. The Sossos remained pagans even after the Almoravid invasion. But a majority of the Mandingoes accepted Islam as their religion in the very earliest days of the Almoravid movement. As Mali blossomed and grew, it became a key region in the Islamic world of the Middle Ages.

Before Mali was able to succeed Ghana as the major kingdom in the western Sudan, the people of Mali first had to meet and overcome the challenge of their pagan rivals, the Sossos. This was no easy task. Led by the powerful and cunning Sumanguru, the Sossos had control of a large amount of Mandingo land.

It would take a man of extraordinary ability, courage, and determination to lead Mali to victory over the Sossos. Fortunately for the Mandingo people, just such a man was available when Mali needed him most. His name was *Sundiata* (sun-di-ah-ta), and he became a legendary figure in his own time and a lasting part of the heritage of West Africa. To this day the descendants of the Mandingo people claim him as their greatest national hero.

"THE HUNGERING LION"

Despite Sundiata's honored place in West African history, no written records about him were kept during his reign. As his story was told and retold down through the centuries, the same story took on many different versions. In time the Sundiata story became completely entangled in legends. Most of these legends are interesting and exciting.

Though the different versions of the Sundiata story varied widely in detail, most of them had a main theme in common. This theme tells of Sundiata's struggles, against great odds, to establish a great Mandingo empire called Mali.

The foundation of the empire of Mali was laid by Sundiata. He led a successful revolt against Sumanguru, the cruel leader of the Sosso. Sumanguru had spared the life of Sundiata when he was a boy.

Sundiata, whose name meant "Hungering Lion," was a prince of the Keita clan. His father was King of Mali. In childhood he seemed tragically misnamed. He was a sickly young fellow afflicted by some form of paralysis. He couldn't even stand up, let alone walk. His mother took him to healers in all parts of the kingdom, but to no avail. The healers all shook their heads sadly and pronounced the lad an incurable invalid.

Strangely enough, Sundiata's fragile health proved to be a blessing in disguise. His father had died while Sundiata was still very young, and control of Mali had fallen to Sumanguru, the powerful King of Sosso.

Sumanguru, as we have already seen, was a cunning as well as a cruel king. He taxed the Malians mercilessly, taking their food, their gold, and the most beautiful of their daughters and wives. Throughout the empire, he was feared and hated. He also saw to it that any potential rivals for his power were ruthlessly eliminated.

According to Mandingo traditions, Sumanguru took one look at the Malian prince named Sundiata and decided to spare the boy's life. Perhaps he was moved to pity because of the boy's sickly health. A more likely explanation was that he couldn't believe that a crippled lad would ever challenge his authority. For Sumanguru, this turned out to be a fatal mistake.

Despite his physical weakness in his early years, Sundiata was an intelligent boy. He had burning ambition and lion-like determination. He refused to give in to the sickness that afflicted him. After many months of almost intolerable suffering he forced himself to walk with the aid of an iron cane. By exercising constantly, he eventually learned to walk without the cane. He grew stronger as he grew older. In time, he completely overcame his lameness. He became an expert horseman and hunter, and his reputation for courage and military skill came to be well known throughout the western Sudan. Gradually the Mandingoes came to look upon Sundiata as the prince who would save them from the tyranny of the Sossos.

In 1230, Sundiata was proclaimed King of Mali. Practically all of the Mandingo leaders rallied around him. In addition, leaders of neighboring groups contributed troops and supplies. Sundiata's army grew stronger.

Eventually the Sosso king, Sumanguru, began to realize that a full-scale revolt was about to take place. He hastened to head off the rebellion. Sumanguru commanded a large and powerful army. In addition, he had convinced his followers that he was protected by extraordinary magical powers which made him invulnerable in battle.

The showdown between the forces of Mali and Sosso came in 1235. Two mighty armies collided head-on near a village called *Karina* (ka-ree-nah). In spite of Sumanguru's supposed magic powers his army was crushed by the forces of Sundiata. Sumanguru himself escaped capture. According to one legend, he was struck by an arrow tipped with a spur of a white rooster. Whereupon Sumanguru simply went poof! and disappeared. (It turned out that arrows tipped with white rooster spurs were just the thing for overcoming Sumanguru's magic.) The legend added that a giant baobab tree sprang up at the spot where Sumanguru vanished.

A less imaginative account of the battle of Karina reported that Sumanguru fled to the mountains to hide after his army was routed. In either case, Sumanguru "disappeared" from history in the sense that his power was totally crushed by the forces of Sundiata. Sumanguru no longer played any part in the history of West Africa after his defeat at Karina.

The triumphant Sundiata went on to conquer and occupy the remainder of Sumanguru's empire. He led his army against the enemy capital, the city of Sosso, which was famous for its 188 strong points. Sosso was considered to be an impregnable fortress, able to resist any attack. After many attacks and many months of fighting, Sundiata's army stormed the city. The Mandingoes, who had suffered terribly under Sumanguru's tyranny, slaughtered the inhabitants of Sosso in cruel revenge.

In 1240, Sundiata or one of his generals completed the destruction of the Sosso Empire by plundering the city of Koumbi, once the great capital of Ghana.

FOUNDATIONS OF EMPIRE

Victory over Sosso left Mali as the most powerful state in the western Sudan. Mali found itself in such a strong position that its leader, Sundiata, could gracefully retire from the wars without ever having known defeat.

The job of extending the boundaries of the new Malian Empire was left to Sundiata's many able followers, including some generals in his army. These generals were appointed as military governors of conquered regions which became new provinces of the empire of Mali. To demonstrate their loyalty to their emperor, the governors sent gifts of rice, millet, arrows, and lances to Sundiata every year.

Sundiata himself devoted his attentions toward laying a firm foundation on which the new empire of Mali could grow and prosper. He moved his capital from Kangaba to *Niani* (ni-ah-ni), the city of his birth. From Niani he worked to re-establish a central government that would provide peace and order throughout the empire.

Years of turmoil and war had completely disrupted the trade and commerce of western Sudan. Now Mali controlled the gold fields of Wangara, and Sundiata quickly saw to it that the profitable trans-Saharan gold-salt trade was restored. In time the golden wealth of Wangara was to mean as much to the prosperity of Mali as it had meant to Ghana.

Another major concern for Sundiata was agriculture. No empire could dream of being powerful as long as it lacked an adequate food supply. Many of Sundiata's soldiers, with no war to fight now, were put to work clearing the land for farming purposes. They practiced a form of "slash and burn agriculture" in which the fields were burned to clear them of grass, bushes, and tree stumps. The newly-cleared farmlands were planted with grains, cotton, calabashes, peanuts, and many other crops. In addition the soldiers-turned-farmers were taught all about the care and feeding of poultry and cattle. This agricultural movement paid off in a few years and Mali became one of the richest farming regions in all of West Africa.

Sundiata, however, did not live to see his empire grow to the height of its power and influence. He died in 1255.

According to one account of his death, Sundiata was fatally wounded by a stray arrow during a celebration

in the city of Niani. According to another account, he died of natural causes. Still another story related that Sundiata drowned in the *Sankarini* (san-kah-ree-ni) River, not far from Niani. Even today, the people of that region conduct special ceremonies to honor the memory of the warrior-founder of the empire of Mali.

Historians are now busy sifting fact from legend in the story of Sundiata. The important thing is that this ruler holds a permanent place in the heritage of the western Sudan. To this day he is a revered folk hero,

Under Sundiata's rule Malians learned much about farming and cattle raising. Mali became one of the richest farming regions in West Africa.

a symbol of courage, wisdom, and all the virtues of greatness. His name is honored in epic poems, in songs, and in the dances.

Sundiata pointed Mali toward the road to power and prosperity. His successors proceeded to establish one of the greatest states that Africa has ever known.

AFTER SUNDIATA

Unlike the pagan empire of Ghana, the new empire of Mali was founded on the Moslem faith. After Sundiata, the rulers of the empire took the proud title of Mansa, which means emperor or sultan.

Sundiata had several sons (the exact number is not known), and one of them named *Wali* (wa-li) succeeded him to the throne. Mansa Wali was known as "the Red King" because his skin was said to have had a copperish tone to it. He was not as spectacular as his father, but he took his job seriously and worked conscientiously to expand the Malian Empire both eastward and westward.

Mansa Wali began the tradition among the ruling Keita clan of being very religious. He made a *hajj*, a holy pilgrimage to the Moslem capital at Mecca on the Arabian peninsula. In this way Wali sought to establish broader contact between his empire in the Sudan and a world across the Sahara.

Mansa Wali ruled from 1255 to 1270. On his death he was succeeded by another of Sundiata's sons, Mansa *Karifa* (ka-ri-fah). Karifa became insane and amused himself by shooting arrows at his subjects!

Mali fell upon sad times. After Karifa, a long period of struggle for power saw a series of rulers of average

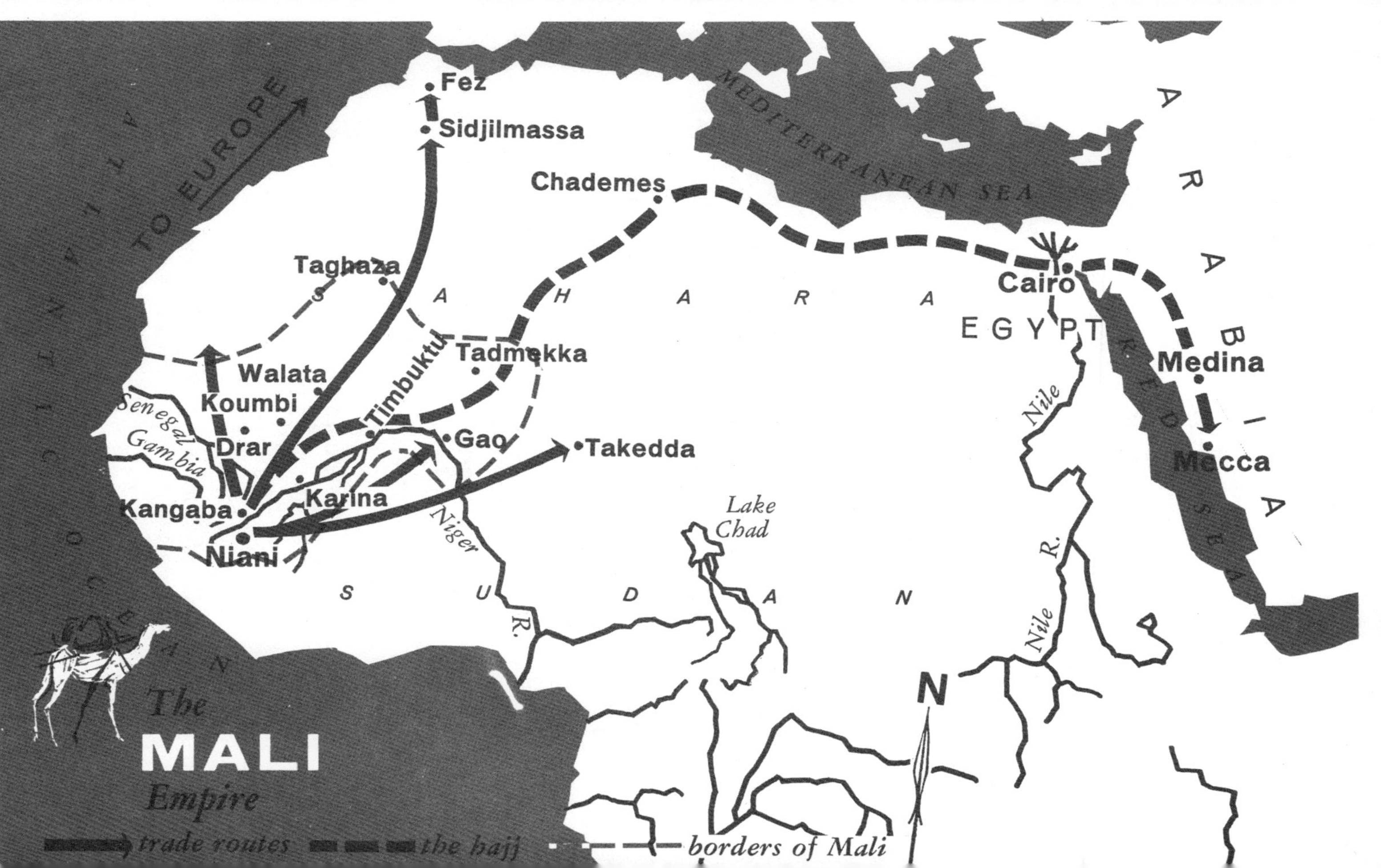

The MALI Empire
trade routes
the hajj
borders of Mali
TO EUROPE
ATLANTIC OCEAN
Fez
Sidjilmassa
Chademes
MEDITERRANEAN SEA
ARABIA
Taghaza
SAHARA
Cairo
EGYPT
Tadmekka
Walata
Koumbi
Timbuktu
Medina
Senegal
Gambia
Drar
Gao
Takedda
Mecca
RED SEA
Kangaba
Karina
Niani
Niger R.
Lake Chad
Nile
Nile R.
SUDAN
N

talent take the throne of Mali. For a time it appeared that the empire founded by Sundiata might never fulfill its great promise.

But once again, when Mali was in desperate need of strong leadership, the right man came onto the scene at the right time. His name was *Musa* (mu-sah). As Mansa Musa I, he became the most famous ruler in the history of the western Sudan.

THE FABULOUS HAJJ

Musa came to the throne of Mali in 1307. He was a grandson of one of Sundiata's sisters. Because his mother's name was Kongo, he is often referred to as Kongo Musa, which means "Moses, son of Kongo." (Musa is the Arabic version of the name Moses.)

He ruled the empire of Mali for twenty-five years. In that quarter of a century the fame of Mali spread across the Sahara to the Middle East, and across the Mediterranean Sea to Europe. Mansa Musa's name was known throughout the world.

Mansa Musa's achievements were many. He extended the boundaries of Mali by diplomacy and war. He promoted trade and commerce. He encouraged the spread of learning. He was a lover of the arts (designs, architecture, literature). Above all Mansa Musa was devoutly religious.

Several of the Moslem rulers of Mali, starting with Mansa Wali, had made pilgrimages to Mecca, the holy

Mansa Musa ruled the empire of Mali for twenty-five years. During that time his name and Mali were known throughout the world.

city of Islam. The hajj, as these pilgrimages are called, is one of the five basic observances of the Islamic faith. If it is possible, every believer in Islam should make this journey to the holy city at least once in his lifetime.

Mansa Musa made his hajj in 1324, in the seventeenth year of his reign. The fact that he made the pilgrimage was not unusual. But the way he made it was.

For Mansa Musa's hajj was one of the grandest grand tours ever recorded. The spectacular wealth displayed by his entourage so dazzled the people on his line of march that their descendants still talked about it one hundred years after it occurred.

As the ruler of the richest empire in West Africa, possibly in the world, at that time, Mansa Musa could easily afford the expenses involved. Even so, it was a hard journey. Arabia, where Mecca is located, was thousands of miles from Musa's capital city, Niani. His caravan would be traveling across some of the most barren wastelands on earth.

Months before the journey, the Mansa's officials and servants went through the empire to collect the necessary food and supplies for the trip. To make sure that the Mansa would have plenty of money, they assembled some 80 to 100 camel-loads of gold dust, each load weighing about 300 pounds.

By the time the caravan was finally assembled, it had become possibly the biggest moving crowd that Africa had ever seen. Mansa Musa was accompanied by thousands of followers. Some sources say that the caravan consisted of 60,000 people!

Included in the entourage were many members of Mansa Musa's family, his close friends, doctors, and teachers, and the most important of the local chiefs of his empire. The Mansa took these chiefs along not only to honor them but to keep them from interfering with his son, whom the Mansa had left behind to rule the empire while he was away.

Mansa Musa's glittering caravan entered Cairo, Egypt, in July 1324, and he was an immediate sensation. The Sultan of Cairo honored the distinguished visitor from the western Sudan with elaborate ceremonies. He spared nothing to make the visitors comfortable. The Sultan even went to the trouble of making preparations for the remainder of the Mansa's journey to Arabia, so that he would be honored and his caravan kept supplied wherever they went.

Mansa Musa's generosity was probably as impressive as his religious faith. He freely gave gifts in the holy cities of Mecca and Medina, and he also gave generously to all those who performed some service for him. On his return trip from Arabia to Mali, Mansa Musa passed through Egypt once more and reportedly "spread the waves of his generosity all over Cairo. There was no one, officer of the court or holder of any official job, who did not receive a sum of gold from him." Indeed, the Mansa was so free with his gifts that two embarrassing things happened.

First, he ran out of money. Even 80 to 100 camel-loads of gold were not enough to keep up with his generous ways. He was forced to borrow from the leading merchants of Cairo. They didn't hesitate to lend money to him because the Mansa was obviously a good credit risk.

And second, the Mansa put so much gold into circulation that he almost ruined the Cairo gold market.

Suddenly gold was not so scarce in Egypt anymore and its price fell sharply. A writer in the service of the Egyptian sultan reported that the Cairo gold market had still not fully recovered from Mansa Musa's visit twelve years after the Musa's hajj.

The enormous prestige that came to Mansa Musa as a result of his fabulous hajj has been well documented. In time the fame of the Emperor of Mali spread to Europe. In the fourteenth century European mapmakers produced a series of charts which marked the position of Mali and depicted the wealth of its emperor.

In an atlas drawn for King Charles V of France, for example, there is a drawing of a Negro monarch wearing robes and a crown and holding a scepter in one hand and a nugget of gold in the other. The inscription reads: "This Negro lord is called Mousse Melly (Musa of Mali), Lord of the Negroes. . . . So abundant is the gold which is found in his country that he is the richest and most noble king of all the land."

King Charles's atlas was drawn in 1375, many years after Mansa Musa's death. But in a sense, Mansa Musa's fame was timeless. He had given the outside world a brief, but dazzling, look at the wealth of Mali. Since his time many people thought of Mali as an Eldorado, a place with an endless supply of gold.

THE POWER AND THE GLORY

At the height of its powers under Mansa Musa, the empire of Mali covered an area about equal to that of Western Europe.

The political subdivisions within Mali were well organized. Some of its territory was under the direct control of the Mansas. In these regions Mali was divided into provinces, just as Ghana had been before it. Each of these provinces were administered by governors called *ferbas* (fur-bas). And each important town in these various provinces had inspectors (or mayors) called *mochrifs* (mo-kreefs). These officials were appointed by the Mansa.

In a region where tribal and family loyalties often run strong, the unusual thing was that these officials seemed completely dedicated to the central government of Mali, headed by the Mansa in Niani. As a result the provinces of Mali were efficiently governed. These provinces were so well policed that merchants and their caravans could travel through them without any fear of robbers and hijackers.

A large area of the Malian Empire was not under the direct rule of the Mansa. These regions were permitted to remain partly independent, so long as the leaders in these regions remained loyal to the Malian emperor. During Mansa Musa's rule, anywhere from thirteen to twenty-four separate Sudanese kingdoms paid allegiance to him. Many of the heads of these kingdoms were local tribal leaders who were left in power with the blessings of the Malian Mansa. Others were appointed by the Emperor of Mali, perhaps as a reward for some outstanding service to the empire.

The fact that the Mansa of Mali did not have direct control over the people of these smaller kingdoms often meant trouble. To prevent some of these rulers from becoming completely independent, the central government at Niani had to keep a sharp eye out for any signs of rebellion.

Just as in Ghana, Mali maintained an enormous army

to keep the peace within the empire and to keep the boundaries safe from attacks by outsiders. Mansa Musa's army was said to number 100,000 men, including 10,000 cavalry troops. The rest were infantrymen—soldiers on foot. A part of the cavalry rode camels while others rode the small and swift Arabian stallions.

While Mansa Musa was away on his long hajj, his army was busy at home extending the boundaries of the Malian Empire. On his trip back home, Mansa Musa was delighted to hear that his soldiers had a "welcome home" gift for him. They had captured the city of *Gao* (ga-ow), capital of the Songhay Kingdom.

Mansa Musa was so elated that he made a special detour to view the captured city. To insure the loyalty of this newly acquired kingdom, Mansa Musa took two of the Songhay princes back to Niani with him, as combination guests and hostages. Many years later, after Mansa Musa's death, these two princes escaped from Niani and returned to Gao, where they founded a new dynasty to challenge the powers of Mali.

FINANCING AN EMPIRE

The financial system of Mali was essentially the same as that of the old Ghanaian Empire except everything was done in a bigger way in Mali. Taxes were still the biggest source of income for the Malian government. Such a system, of course, required prosperous trade and commerce. Through the Mansa's representatives, the taxes were efficiently collected.

From all accounts, Mali was a land of plenty—plenty of everything. On the fertile soil of Mali, farmers grew sorghum, rice, taro, yams, beans, and onions. They raised poultry, cattle, sheep, and goats. And there was plenty of game meat around, such as a nice tasty hippopotamus steak. Those who didn't like hippopotamus meat could substitute wild buffalo, elephant, or crocodile. The wild animals were killed with spears and poisoned arrows.

In addition to food crops, cotton was also grown in many parts of Mali and great quantities of cotton cloth were available for clothing. One of the most useful noncultivated plants was the baobab tree, which gave a white meal for breadmaking, a medicinal liquid, and a red dye.

The industrious people of Mali skillfully put their country's resources to use. Every large city or middle-sized village had its own craftsmen, woodcarvers, silversmiths, goldsmiths, coppersmiths, blacksmiths, weavers, tanners, and dyers.

But the greatest source of income for the government of Mali was neither agriculture nor manufacturing. It was trade. Having replaced Ghana as the greatest power of the western Sudan, Mali also took over the trans-Saharan gold-salt trade.

To protect the important trade routes between the Maghreb and the western Sudan, Mansa Musa established friendly commercial relations with the Sultan of Fez in Morocco. By this time the empire of Mali and Morocco were practically next-door neighbors. Mali's boundaries had pushed far enough northward to include Taghaza and its salt mines (which were well outside the borders of the old Ghanaian Empire).

In the gold-producing regions to the south, however, Mali had the same difficulties as Ghana in trying to gain complete control over the Wangara gold miners. The

The people of Mali had plenty to eat. Hunters used spears and poisoned arrows to kill many kinds of animals for food.

people of Wangara were apparently expert jungle fighters. In addition, the tsetse flies in the forest belt were disastrous for the horses of the Malian cavalry. The result was that nobody could tell the Wangara people what to do or what not to do.

Mali, like Ghana, controlled Wangara's gold output.

By the time of Mansa Musa, the western Sudan of Africa was already the most important source of gold for Europe. And these Sudanese gold mines would remain Europe's major source of the precious metal until the discovery of the "New World" across the Atlantic Ocean.

In a very significant way, Mali's external trade (trade with other countries) differed from that of Ghana. In Ghana's time gold and other trade goods from the western Sudan moved northward to the Maghreb and, through there, to the countries in Europe on the other side of the Mediterranean Sea.

In the days of Mali, a second major trading route was established. This one pushed off north and east across the Sahara to Tunis and Cairo, Egypt. Gradually the northeast trade route became the main one. This development started a new era in which the influence of Egypt began to play an important role in the western Sudan.

Mansa Musa's fabulous pilgrimage undoubtedly gave a tremendous boost to this economic and cultural exchange between Mali and Egypt. Historian Charles Monteil wrote:

"Egyptians came there in numerous caravans every year. . . . In Mali itself, these foreigners had an influence which was all the greater since the Mansa drew large tax revenues from them which he levied under diverse forms."

There was another reason for Mali's push to the east and it was a source of wealth that was as important as the gold of Wangara or the salt of Taghaza. This source of wealth was the copper mines at *Takedda* (ta-

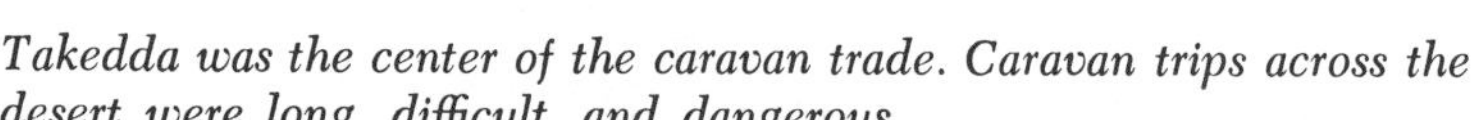

Takedda was the center of the caravan trade. Caravan trips across the desert were long, difficult, and dangerous.

kay-dah), about 250 miles east of Gao. Many parts of North Africa, from the Maghreb to Egypt, drew their supply of this useful metal from the mines of Takedda. Mansa Musa himself once remarked that the copper mines at Takedda were his most important source of revenue.

Takedda was also a thriving center of the caravan trade. According to Arab writers, an enormous caravan

of 12,000 camels passed through Takedda each year. This illustrates the considerable amount of trading that went on between Niani and Cairo.

The cross-desert journey was long, always hard, and often dangerous. Yet the caravans kept coming in greater numbers because the profits from trade in Mali apparently made it worth the effort and risk. Arab travelers reported that even the common people of Mali seemed to be well-off. They marveled that some of the Malian households were lighted at night by candles, which were not common items in those days.

CITIES OF MALI

In an empire as large as Mali, many important commercial centers developed and prospered. Most of these centers owed their commercial success to their locations. The Malian capital of Niani, for example, was one of these fortunate cities which sat in the center of a vast network of caravan trails. The trade routes out of Niani headed off in all directions—to Egypt, *Angila* (an-gee-lah), *Akadamer* (Ak-a-da-mah), Fez, *Sus* (Soos), Sidjilmassa, *Taut* (ta-oot), Drar, and the *Fezzan* (fez-zan).

Arab writers described Niani as the "great metropole" of the western Sudan, a large city of great palaces. Located perhaps about ten miles from the Sankarini River (a tributary of the Niger), Niani was said to be as long as it was wide. Unfortunately no one went to the trouble of recording just how long and wide that was.

As the capital of the empire, Niani (like Koumbi before it) was the seat of the Mansa's royal court and government. Almost daily the city served as a setting for magnificent ceremonies and pageants.

But Niani was not the only great city of Mali. Other cities matched it in commercial activities and often surpassed it as centers of learning. Once more, trade and commerce had brought an exchange of ideas, books, and scholars. Culture and scholarship flourished in the luxury and security of Mali's great commercial centers.

In many cities of the empire of Mali, trade, commerce and learning flourished. Young people had opportunity to talk with great scholars.

There was *Walata* (wa-la-tah), founded by people who fled Koumbi during the Sosso conquest and occupation. Walata later replaced Koumbi as the gateway to the Sudan for the trans-Saharan caravans coming from the Maghreb.

There was Gao, downstream on the Niger, which was to become the great capital of the Songhay Empire.

There was Timbuktu, sitting at the Great Bend of the Niger, between Niani and Gao. Timbuktu's location put it right at the spot where the people of the desert and the people of the river traditionally met for trade. In due course Timbuktu grew from a tent settlement to a great center of commerce and learning. It had no equal in western Sudan. The city was to reach the height of its glory during the days of the Songhay Empire. (We will take a closer look at Timbuktu in the next chapter.)

The great Mansa Musa the First left his mark on many of the great cities of his empire. During his pilgrimage to Mecca, he met a great Arab scholar named *Es-Saheli* (es-sa-he-li) who was a poet and an outstanding architect. The persuasive Mansa Musa talked Es-Saheli into returning to Mali with him.

On his return trip from Mecca, Mansa Musa inspected Gao, which had been added to his empire while he was away. He was disappointed to discover that an undistinguished structure there was being used as the mosque—a temple or church in the Islamic religion. He gave Es-Saheli his first assignment—to build a more suitable structure where Moslems could worship.

Es-Saheli did such an outstanding job that the Mansa Musa later had him design an auditorium in Niani. Later, Es-Saheli also designed a royal residence and a mosque in Timbuktu. His work won him lasting fame throughout the Moslem world (the foundation of the mosque at Gao still survives). For many years after he died in Timbuktu, travelers to that city stopped to view his grave and show their respect.

In addition to Niani, Timbuktu, Walata, and Gao, one other city in the western Sudan deserves mention. This was *Jenne* (jen), which also won fame as a commercial center and the home of many noted Negro scholars. Though Jenne was a small city compared to Niani or Timbuktu, and though it was located only a few days' march from Niani, Jenne was never captured by the empire of Mali.

It has been said that Jenne was assaulted ninety-nine times by the various emperors of Mali. The people of Jenne were determined to maintain their independence from outside control, and they turned back all attacks.

THE DECLINE OF MALI

On his return from the pilgrimage to Mecca in 1325, Musa had hoped to wind up his affairs at home and put his son in control so that he could go back to Arabia to spend the remainder of his life in meditation near the holy city. Mansa Musa never realized this wish. One thing or another kept him at home. He never went to Mecca again.

Mansa Musa I died in 1332. His reign lasted twenty-five years. His influence and prestige had been so great that many historians have come to identify the story of the western Sudan during the fourteenth century as "the century of Musa."

Mansa Musa was succeeded on the throne of Mali by his son, *Maghan* (ma-gan). Unfortunately Mansa Maghan had neither his father's ability nor his wisdom. Because of his poor ability, Mali suffered two important setbacks.

The first setback was the loss of Timbuktu. Warlike *Mossi* (mo-si) people from the region of the Volta River raided Timbuktu shortly after Maghan became king. The Mossi routed the Mandingo garrison defending the city and set Timbuktu afire.

Following the Timbuktu disaster, Mali suffered the second setback. Maghan permitted the two Songhay princes, whom his father had brought back from Gao as hostages, to escape. These two princes went back home to Gao, where they founded a new Songhay dynasty. Efforts by Mali to disrupt the new Songhay regime were unsuccessful. Eventually the rulers in Gao were to replace Mali as the supreme power in the western Sudan.

Mansa Maghan ruled only four years. On his death he was succeeded by his uncle (Mansa Musa's brother), Sulayman. Mansa Sulayman did much to repair the damages done by Maghan.

In 1351, Mansa Sulayman followed his brother's example and went on a pilgrimage to Mecca. He took this opportunity to reassert Malian control in the east. Gao, however, remained outside of Mali's control.

Mansa Sulayman died in 1359. He was the last of the able Mandingo emperors. His successors were weak men, who could not hold the vast empire together. At the same time, the power of the Songhay Empire, centered in the city of Gao, grew with the years. Sometime around 1475, Songhay passed Mali as the most powerful and important state in the western Sudan.

In 1481, Mali made one last bid to fight off the challenge of Songhay. The Malians established the first direct Sudanese contact with Europeans through Portuguese sailors who had arrived on Mali's Atlantic coast. Mali sought an alliance with the Europeans to hold back the Songhay advance from the east.

The alliance was never made, and Mali's fate was sealed. Mali lingered on for nearly two centuries more, but it was a mere shadow of its former glory.

CHAPTER 3 SONGHAY

The Rise of Gao

It is no accident that many of the world's earliest civilizations began near great river systems. The Nile River played a very important part in the development of the Egyptian civilization. The Indus and Hwang Rivers played major roles in shaping the civilizations of India and China. The Niger River played a similar role in the development of African civilization.

Great river systems were important in the birth of civilizations for many reasons. One important reason was that the rivers were a method of transportation (when people could travel on the rivers, they were able to meet and exchange ideas with many other groups of people). Another important reason was that the soil near these rivers was fertile—very good for growing crops.

The Middle Niger, from Lake Debo around the Great Bend downstream to Busa, formed a navigable waterway approximately one thousand miles long on which boats could easily sail. Along its entire length are countless islands and inlets, narrow bays of water cutting into the land. At both ends of the waterway, there were rapids (where the current is strong and there are many obstacles), which helped to make the area easily defended against invaders who came by water.

To the people who settled here long ago, the Niger was known as *Isa Beri* (ee-sa beh-ri), the "great river."

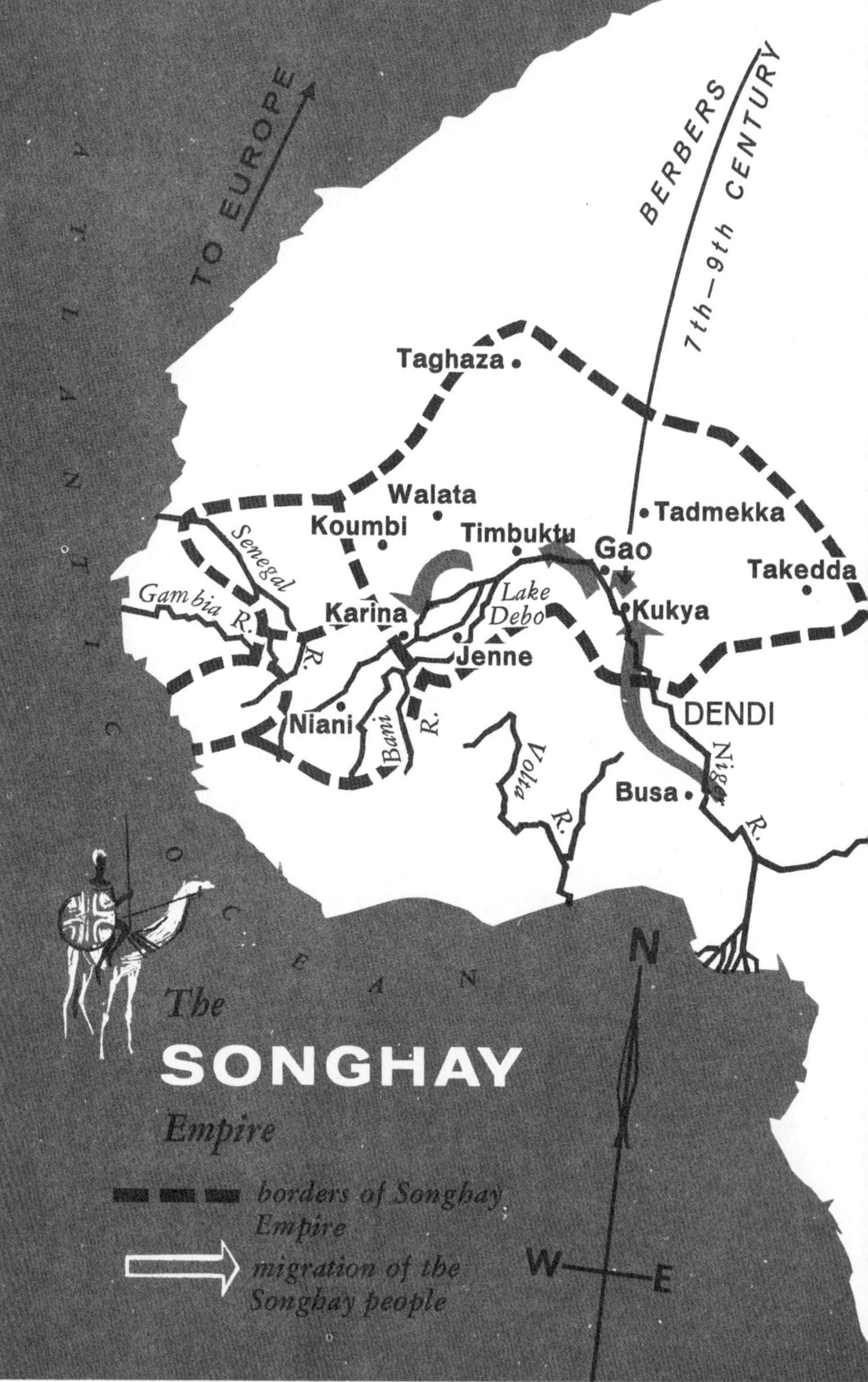

TO EUROPE
BERBERS
7th—9th CENTURY
ATLANTIC OCEAN
Taghaza
Walata
Koumbi
Timbuktu
Tadmekka
Gao
Takedda
Senegal R.
Gambia R.
Karina
Lake Debo
Kukya
Jenne
DENDI
Niani
Bani R.
Volta R.
Niger R.
Busa
N
W
E
The SONGHAY Empire
borders of Songhay Empire
migration of the Songhay people

When the Niger overflowed it left behind fertile layers of topsoil. The flooded region was especially rich for fishing and hunting. Cattle thrived on the grass growing along the riverbanks. The trunks of the fan palm trees which grew here were used in the making of canoes.

A prized piece of Sudanese real estate, the Middle Niger was the traditional home of the Songhay people. To this day the Songhay (numbering perhaps a half million or more people now) still live in this area, tilling the soil, raising cattle and practicing crafts as they have done since a time before recorded history.

The years have obscured or hidden the origin of these Songhay people. In the dimly remembered past the Middle Niger area was said to have been occupied by people who were divided into "masters of the river" and "masters of the soil." Later other people entered the region and mingled with the people who were already there.

The Songhay then were a people of farmers, fishermen, hunters, craftsmen, traders, and warriors—a confederation of people who came to dominate the Middle Niger and its surrounding area. Starting perhaps around the region of *Dendi* (den-dee), they gradually pushed their way upstream.

The first large Songhay settlement was a town called *Kukya* (kook-yah), in Dendi country, near what is now the northwest frontier of Nigeria. Kukya grew and prospered during an early period of peace. It became the Songhay capital and it attracted people from the surrounding regions. Eventually it also attracted invaders from more distant places.

Sometime between the seventh and ninth centuries a group of Berber nomads (people who wander from

place to place) swept out of the deserts from the north. They captured Kukya and promptly set up a ruling group that has come to be known as the *Dia* (dee-ah) kings.

Some of the Songhay people did not like the new rulers. They pushed off farther upstream on the Niger to found a settlement which became the town of Gao. But the Dia rulers were not to be denied that easily.

The people of the Middle Niger area were divided into two groups—masters of the river and masters of the soil. The masters of the river were experts at navigating the Niger River.

They, too, extended their control upstream. Soon Gao also came under the control of the Dia kings.

In time, Gao became the most important settlement in the region. While Kukya remained the traditional fortified capital of the region, Gao became its foremost commercial center. Caravans wound their way to Gao from Egypt and North Africa.

Like Koumbi in the ancient empire of Ghana, Gao

was divided into two separate sections. One of them was inhabited mostly by Moslem traders and the other mostly by the local Songhay people.

ISLAM COMES TO GAO

Through frequent intermarriages the Berber Dia line of kings became almost indistinguishable from the local Negroes. Over the years the rulers also adopted the customs of their subjects, including the worship of the traditional Songhay gods.

Near the beginning of the eleventh century, as more and more Moslem traders settled in Gao, and as Gao took on an ever-increasing importance to Songhay, a significant development occurred. A Dia king named *Kossoi* (kos-so-ee) was converted to Islam in 1009, probably at the request of the Moslem merchants of Gao. Also, he consented to reside in Gao at least part of each year. The presence of the Dia ruler in the city gave it a new prestige and military protection from raids by other roving bands of nomads. From the eleventh century on, Gao became a "commercial metropole, habitual residence of the Songhay royal court, and center of the Moslems."

At the beginning the conversion of the Dia rulers to Islam included only their families, and some of the leading officials of the royal court. The majority of the Songhay people continued to worship their own traditional gods. Nevertheless, the fact that the Songhay chiefs were Moslems helped to speed the spread of Islam through the western Sudan. From the time of Dia Kossoi, it became a tradition that only Moslems were to occupy the throne of Songhay.

SONGHAY AGAINST MALI

From the eleventh through the fourteenth centuries, Songhay's biggest problem was the maintenance of its freedom and independence from the growing powers of the neighboring empire of Mali. Gao moved in and out of Mali's control throughout much of the fourteenth and fifteenth centuries.

You may recall from the last chapter that Mali's invading armies captured Gao during the fourteenth century—in 1325—while Mansa Musa was on his famous hajj to Mecca. Judging from the importance that Mansa Musa attached to the capture of Gao, Songhay was regarded as a prosperous addition to Mali's domain.

Mansa Musa returned from his hajj by way of Gao to see the city and its king, who was named *Dia Assibai* (dee-ah as-see-ba-ee). Mansa Musa took two of Assibai's sons back to Niani with him as hostages to make sure that the Dia would think carefully before trying to rebel. The two Songhay princes were *Ali Kolon* (ah-lee ko-lon) and *Sulayman Nar* (su-lay-man nar).

Ali Kolon was a fine soldier and leader. Mansa Musa decided that he might as well put Ali Kolon to work. But while he was making himself useful to the Mansa of Mali, the Songhay prince was making plans of his own.

Prince Ali Kolon led many military expeditions for the empire of Mali. No one seemed to attach any significance to the fact that each of his trips took him a little closer to the area where his family lived. But Ali Kolon knew what he was doing. Secretly he hid arms and provisions along a route that he would one day use for his escape back to the city of Gao.

Mansa Musa died in 1332, and he was succeeded on the throne of Mali by his weak son, Maghan. At this

After the death of Mansa Musa, Ali Kolon and Sulayman Nar escaped from Niani. They returned to Gao where Ali founded the Sunni dynasty. This dynasty made Songhay great.

point Ali Kolon decided that the time for his break had come. With his brother Sulayman Nar and a few supporters, he made a dash on horseback to his home in Gao. A furious Mansa Maghan ordered troops to capture the escaping Songhay princes, but the brothers evaded them.

While Ali Kolon was in Gao, his father Assibai had died, and four other kings had taken the throne of Gao. Now Ali Kolon was back to claim his inheritance. He promptly saw to it that he was elected the new chief of Gao, and he replaced the last of the Dia line. He then founded a new dynasty, or succession of rulers, called *Sunni* (soon-ni), which means "replacement."

Ali Kolon and his successors in the Sunni line established a firm hold in Gao. They turned back every effort by the rulers of Mali to take their power and to bring Gao back into Mali's fold. But the Sunni rulers themselves had little luck at first in trying to extend their own powers much beyond the city limits of Gao itself. For most of the fourteenth century and the early part of the fifteenth century, Mali and Songhay were forced to live with each other in a sort of restless peace.

But time was working on the side of Songhay. As Mali's strength declined, Songhay gradually emerged as the major power in the western Sudan.

The ruler who raised Songhay into its new position was one of the fiercest warrior kings ever to appear on the African scene. His name was Ali, and he is remembered in history as *Sunni Ali Ber* (soon-ni ah-lee beer). Sunni is the name of the dynasty, and Ali Ber means Ali the Great. He came to the throne in 1464.

THE CAPTURE OF TIMBUKTU

The chain of conquests which forged a great Songhay Empire began with the capture of Timbuktu around the year 1468. Perhaps the word "recaptured" should be used. Timbuktu was probably founded by the people of the Niger, and it was traditionally regarded as a Songhay city. On the Great Bend of the Niger River, it was a place where the people of the river came to trade with the nomads of the desert.

During the years of the empire of Mali, Timbuktu was already a center of commerce and one of the major

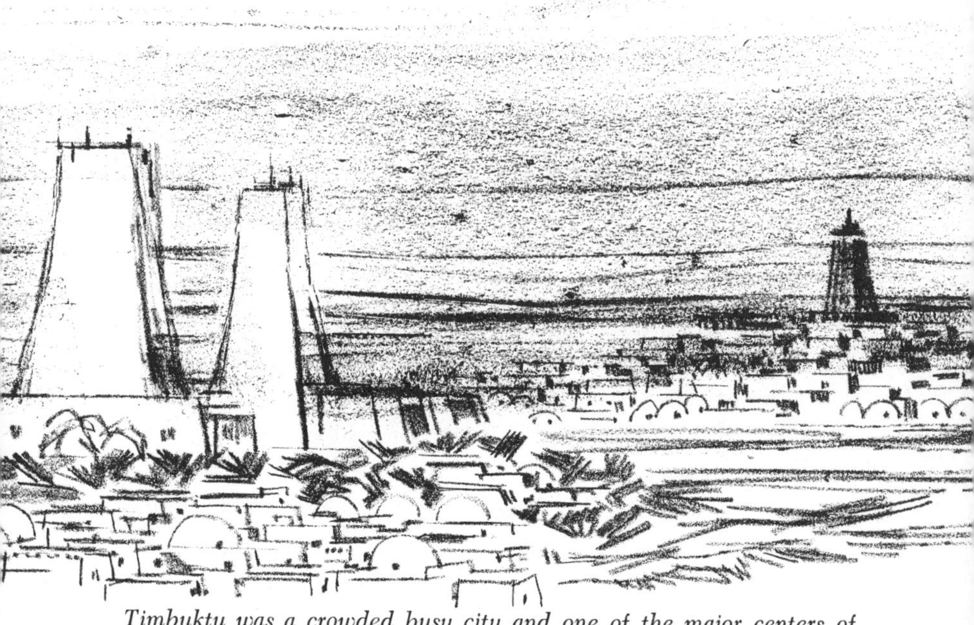

Timbuktu was a crowded busy city and one of the major centers of learning in Africa. It was proud of its great university.

centers of learning in all of Africa. It is no wonder that it was a prized possession of Mali. It had a great university, *Sankore* (san-ko-ray), which attracted many students from distant parts of Africa. Scholarship and commerce were the glories of Timbuktu.

Timbuktu was a crowded and fairly drab-looking town. Except for a mosque and a palace (built for Mansa Musa by Es-Saheli, the poet-architect), the town was said to be little more than "a mass of ill-looking houses, built of mud-bricks."

Mali's hold on Timbuktu weakened after the death of Mansa Musa. Around 1433 the city was invaded by Tuareg nomads from the desert. Their leader was a chief named *Akil* (ah-keel).

Though Timbuktu was his, Chief Akil chose not to live there. Instead he remained in the desert and appointed a man named *Ammar* (am-mar) to represent him in Timbuktu. One of Ammar's duties was to collect taxes. He kept one third of the money himself and turned two thirds over to Chief Akil.

When Ammar heard of the growing strength of the Sunni rulers of Songhay, he unwisely sent a letter to Sunni Ali Ber in Gao and boasted that Timbuktu could repulse any attack. Later he was sorry about this letter.

To Ammar's dismay, his own chief made a habit of double-crossing him regularly. Every time that Ammar had completed his tax collection, Chief Akil would ride into town to seize all the tax money, including the one third that was supposed to go to Ammar. He plotted to get even with Akil. To do so he needed the help of his old enemy in Gao, Sunni Ali Ber.

Ammar sent a secret message to Sunni Ali Ber, offering to hand the city over to the Songhay king if he would come and drive off Chief Akil. Ammar hoped that Sunni Ali Ber would forget about the boastful letter, and reward him for his plan.

Regardless of what he thought about Ammar, Sunni Ali Ber was not going to let an opportunity like this slip by. He ordered his army to march at once on Timbuktu. Sunni Ali Ber himself rode at the head of his cavalry.

The Songhay army moved along the bank of the Niger. When they reached a city which was a "suburb" of Timbuktu, they were seen by Chief Akil and Ammar, who were watching from a hilltop.

The sight of the huge army from Songhay so unnerved Akil that he decided to flee. Many of the Sankore teachers also left as soon as they could. The Sankore scholars had loudly scorned the people of Songhay as something on the level of uncouth savages. Now that the Songhay army was on Timbuktu's shores, the timid scholars were not going to test the anger of the people whom they had insulted.

Ammar himself started to carry through with his part of the treacherous bargain. He sent canoes to the Songhay army to help them cross the river. When Sunni Ali Ber stepped onto the shore, Ammar suddenly panicked. Perhaps he remembered the letter that he had sent. Or perhaps he recalled that the Songhay people had a low regard for traitors of any kind. In any case, Ammar, too, left town.

The Songhay army plundered Timbuktu and slew hundreds of its citizens. Sunni Ali was especially cruel to those accused of having traded with the Tuaregs. For Sunni Ali considered the Tuaregs his bitterest enemies. This was the result of decades of Tuareg-Songhay rivalry for control of the Middle Niger.

In a famous history of the Sudan, the historian *Es-Sadi* (es-sah-di) described Sunni Ali as a "master tyrant" and "scoundrel." Like many other Moslem writers, Es-Sadi could never forgive Sunni Ali for his cruel and humiliating treatment of the Moslem scholars of Timbuktu, especially since the Songhay king was supposed to be a Moslem himself. Almost without exception Moslem historians tended to heap scorn on Sunni Ali.

Yet there was no doubt that Sunni Ali was revered by his own people. They called him "the most high," implying that he was like a god. His ability on the battlefield humbled those who stood against him. Because he was headstrong, he was often unpredictable.

If he was cruel, he was also generous. Above all else Sunni Ali was an able ruler with a real talent for organization and government.

THE FIGHT FOR JENNE

Having taken Timbuktu, Sunni Ali turned his attentions to another great city in Africa named Jenne.

This city was founded sometime in the thirteenth century by the Soninkes in the declining years of Ghana's empire. The founders of Jenne had picked the site well.

Jenne was set in the backwaters of the Bani River, a tributary of the Niger. It was some 300 miles southwest of Timbuktu.

The approaches to Jenne were protected by treacherous swamps. It could be reached only by way of narrow, twisting canals and streams. This made Jenne easily defendable against invaders. You may recall from the previous chapter that the kings of Mali made 99 attempts to capture Jenne, only to give up in the end in frustration.

Learning flourished within Jenne. It had a university of very high reputation. The university boasted of having thousands of teachers who lectured and conducted research on many subjects, including medicine. There were reports of several difficult surgical operations successfully performed by the medical doctors of Jenne.

Though Timbuktu was better known to a world outside of the western Sudan, Jenne was reputed to be far more beautiful. Jenne's attractiveness was due to the beauty of the waterways around the city and to the imaginative designs of many of its buildings.

Jenne was a beautiful city and an important trading place for caravans from all parts of Africa. Its university had a very high reputation.

Jenne was also a match for Timbuktu as a commercial center. One reason for Timbuktu's commercial success was that many caravans had to pass through Timbuktu to get to Jenne.

Sunni Ali soon realized that the capture of Jenne was not going to be easy. Instead of trying to take Jenne by direct attack, Sunni Ali and his men settled down around the town. They hoped to starve Jenne into surrender. Neither side could know at the beginning just how long this siege would last.

It went on for seven years, seven months, and seven days.

The soggy land around Jenne turned the siege into a kind of amphibious (both land and sea) operation. The army of Sunni Ali Ber had to constantly shift positions according to the season. During the summer dry seasons, the Songhay army camped around and just outside of Jenne to cut off all land traffic to and from the town. But during the winter wet season when the floods came and water surrounded Jenne on all sides, the Songhay army was obliged to pull back to higher ground. Sunni Ali had a "fleet" of some 400 canoes to blockade Jenne, cutting off all the water approaches by which supplies might enter that city.

While the wet season lasted, the Songhay troops actually did little fighting. They were too busy cultivating the soil around the camps so that they would have something to eat. But once the floodwaters receded, the Songhay army moved back into position around Jenne.

After seven years, Sunni Ali and his troops had reached the limit of their endurance. Many of the Songhay officers advised their king to give up this attempt to capture Jenne.

Sunni Ali was almost ready to quit when he received a secret message from a captain of the army defending Jenne. The message told the Songhay king that Jenne was suffering from famine and that its defenses were ready to collapse. Now it was a question of which side could outlast the other for just a little while longer.

Sunni Ali ordered his men to hang on for one last push. He increased the guard around Jenne to make sure that no food or other supplies could reach the desperate town. After several more months of stubborn resistance, the ruling council in Jenne had had enough. Knowing that Jenne's condition was hopeless, the council decided to deliver the town to the Songhay king.

The King of Jenne rode into the Songhay camp to surrender to Sunni Ali. Sunni Ali greeted the young King of Jenne with great respect, inviting him to sit at the side of the Songhay monarch. At this time a tradition began, and it gave the kings of Jenne the privilege of sitting on the same mat as the kings of Songhay, a sign of mutual regard between the rulers of the two lands.

Sunni Ali marched into Jenne at the head of his

It took seven years of fighting for Sunni Ali to make the king of Jenne surrender. This so impressed Sunni Ali that he invited the king of Jenne to sit beside him on the throne.

army. But those who expected Jenne to share the same fate as Timbuktu were pleasantly surprised. The Songhay troops did not pillage the town. Perhaps the Songhay army was too tired and worn out.

A more likely explanation, however, was that the Songhay people have always admired courage. Songhay contempt for the cowardice of the people of Timbuktu might have been partly responsible for the terrible slaughter that resulted after Timbuktu's capture.

Jenne, on the other hand, had put up a heroic defense through years of hardship. For all the trouble that Jenne had caused him, Sunni Ali went out of his way to show the people that he held no grudge. He was generous in victory, and extremely kind to all. To seal the bond between the conquerors and the conquered, Sunni Ali married the Queen-Mother of Jenne, the mother of the young king.

The year of the capture of Jenne has been set as 1473. Shortly after the addition of Jenne, the Songhay Empire replaced its long-time rival, Mali, as the dominant power in the western Sudan.

THE REALM OF SUNNI ALI

Sunni Ali's goal was not to destroy the empire of Mali, but to take it intact. Like the kings of England in the Middle Ages, he was constantly on one campaign or another. These expeditions kept him on the go so much that he maintained royal living quarters at half a dozen places.

Though Sunni Ali appeared to be constantly on the move, he maintained strong central control. Following the example of Mali, he divided his empire into prov-

Prince Henry the Navigator directed the establishment of Portuguese trading posts on the coasts of Africa.

inces and placed each under the control of a governor. He understood the importance of the Niger River in commerce and in military operations.

By Sunni Ali's time, the size of trade along the eastern trans-Saharan route, described in the last chapter, was reaching a peak. Gao had grown into a town of perhaps 10,000 people and a highly important market center. Two hundred and fifty miles northeast of Gao was another commercial center. Also to the east was Takedda, the industrial, copper mining town which served Mansa Musa so well and was now doing the same for the empire of Sunni Ali.

At this time the people of the western Sudan were beginning to meet new visitors, the Portuguese. Directed by Portugal's famed hero of exploration, Prince Henry the Navigator, Portuguese ships and sailors traveled down the west coast of Africa, establishing a number of coastal trading posts.

The Portuguese came in direct contact with the Mandingoes of Mali, who sought an alliance with the Europeans to strengthen Mandingo power against the rising challenge of Songhay. Sometime later, the Portuguese obtained permission from Sunni Ali to send a mission to Timbuktu. But from available records, nothing came of that.

European explorers and traders seeking to get into the Sudan from the coastal regions found their way barred by swamp-infested rain forests. Raids to get slaves had brought distrust and hostility from the Sudanese people.

Though the Portuguese established some control along the coast and in regions south of the Sudan, the interior regions of the western Sudan remained, by and large, an area "off limits" to European visitors through the fifteenth and sixteenth centuries.

THE WAYS OF THE SONGHAY

The social system in Songhay had many aspects of a caste system, that is, a person's social and economic standing depended largely on what group or tribe he belonged to. If he belonged to a particular group, it often determined what sort of work he did and with whom he associated.

There were special castes whose members specialized in caring for horses. Another caste did most of the smithing, particularly the job of making spears and arrows for the Songhay army. In the lake districts west of Timbuktu, there was a caste of fishermen who transported people and goods at the command of the ruler. Members of other castes and tribes attended to the personal needs of the king, his family, and his court.

At the top of the social and political ladder were the descendants of the original Songhay people of Kukya. They enjoyed special privileges and were kept apart from the general population. They were not allowed to marry outside of their own caste.

Next in line were the freemen and traders of the cities and town, and the members of the army, composed of noble cavalrymen, and foot soldiers. A large portion of the infantry was made up of war prisoners.

The Songhay army represented something of an innovation for the western Sudan. Up to this time Sudanese armies had been raised by giving each province a quota for providing a certain number of soldiers. Any male citizen of the empire who was healthy could be drafted into military service. If this citizen happened to be a farmer, his fields would be left to the weeds while he was away.

The Songhay Empire eliminated the waste caused by drafting people with civilian occupations. They organized a completely professional army. Members of the Songhay army were expected to fight the wars of the empire, and that was all. In Sunni Ali's time, that was enough to keep them busy all the time.

The Songhay army lived in barracks and camps separated from the civilian population. The mounted soldiers (those who rode horses or camels) were armed with sabres and lances and wore breastplates padded with cotton, for protection. The foot soldiers fought with long, pointed staves and with bow and poison-tipped arrows.

At the bottom of the social scale in Songhay were the war captives and slaves who were not placed in the army but put to work on the farms. Some of the "farms" were rather like labor camps.

Through the fifteenth century most of the Songhay people continued to worship tribal gods, though the kings were Moslems. Sunni Ali practiced the Moslem faith, but not very sincerely. There were reports that Sunni Ali refused to say his five daily prayers at the appointed times. Instead he said all five prayers together in the evening. On occasion he merely recited the names of the prayers without bothering to recite them in full.

His treatment of the Moslem doctors in Timbuktu was evidence that he felt no particular bond of kinship to another person simply because the other person was also a Moslem.

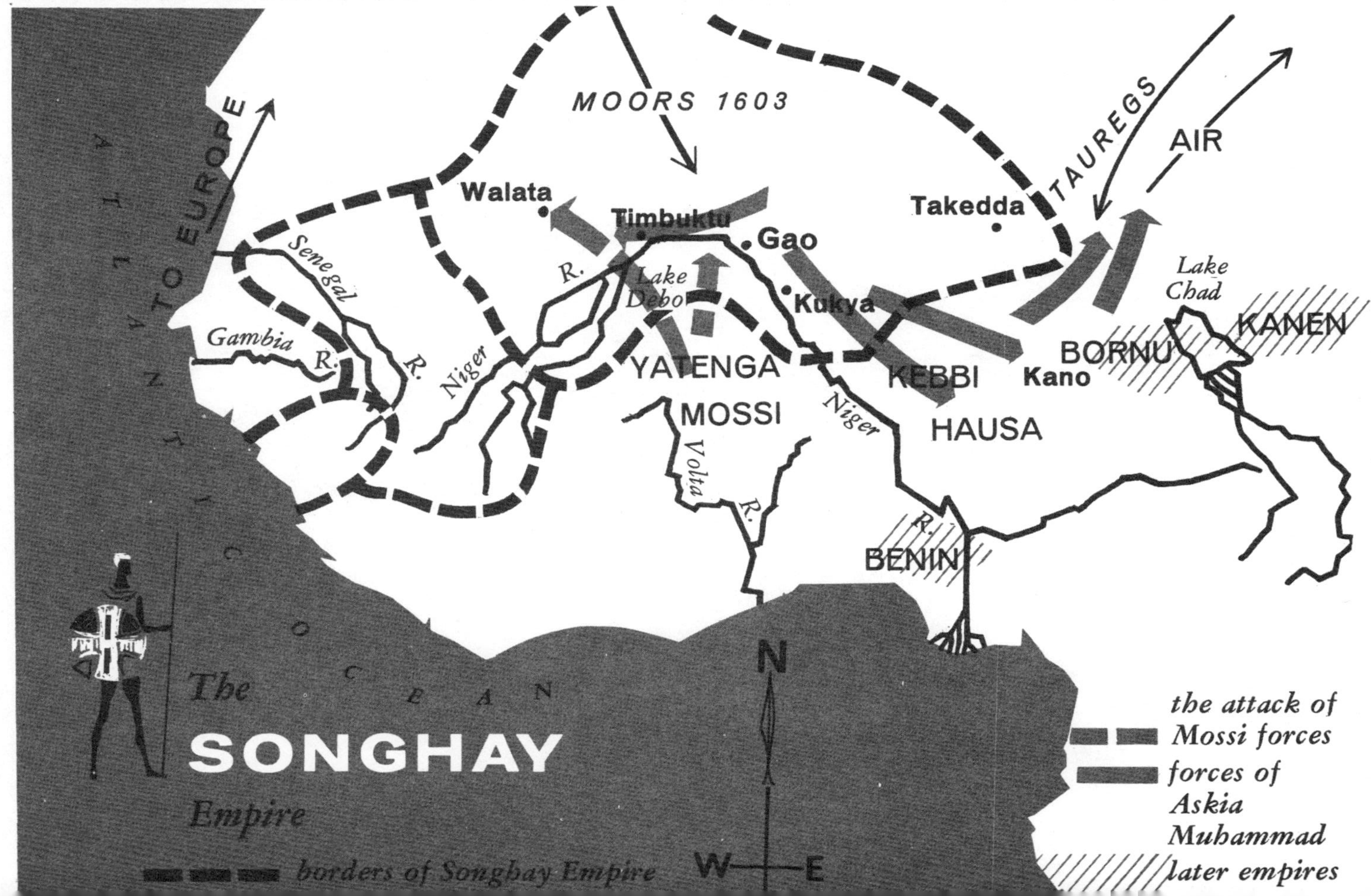

The SONGHAY Empire
MOORS 1603
TAUREGS
AIR
TO EUROPE
ATLANTIC OCEAN
Walata
Timbuktu
Gao
Takedda
Kukya
Lake Debo
Lake Chad
Senegal R.
Gambia R.
Niger R.
Niger
Volta R.
R.
YATENGA
MOSSI
KEBBI
Kano
BORNU
KANEN
HAUSA
BENIN
N
W
E
borders of Songhay Empire
the attack of Mossi forces
forces of Askia Muhammad
later empires

SUNNI ALI'S LAST CAMPAIGNS

Around 1480 the daring warlike Mossi people from *Yatenga* (ya-ting-ga), near the Volta River, broke through the Songhay lines and marched northwest into the desert. There they attacked the town of Walata, which fell after a month-long siege. The Mossi sacked Walata, taking many women and children as captives.

To move his own army to Walata, Sunni Ali thought of a fantastic engineering project. He wanted to build a canal from Lake Debo, west of Timbuktu, to Walata, a distance of some 150 miles. He was determined to have a waterway as a supply line for his military activities in Walata.

We will never know whether or not Sunni Ali could have accomplished this amazing job of canal-building. The project was barely started when the Songhay king learned that the Mossi had left Walata and were now threatening to attack his forces from the rear. Sunni Ali abandoned the canal project, turned his forces around, and drove back the Mossi. Because of the fighting abilities of the Mossi, he was never able to crush the Mossi army.

Sunni Ali's rule was coming to an end. In 1492, the year that Christopher Columbus discovered a "new world" across the Atlantic Ocean, Sunni Ali died after ruling the Songhay Empire for nearly twenty-eight years. Ali was said to have drowned while crossing a stream on his way back to Gao.

In death as in life, the career of Sunni Ali bore many resemblances to that of Mali's Sundiata. Both of these rulers were fearless warriors who prepared the foundations for great empires. They were hated by those who opposed and fought against them, and they were loved and revered by their own people. Their strong personalities dominated the western Sudan during their own time. Finally, both of them left lasting impressions on the pages of history.

ASKIA THE GREAT

Sunni Ali's immediate successor to the throne of Songhay was his son. Like his father the new king seemed to be a Moslem in name only. He too worshipped the traditional gods.

The learned Moslems living within Songhay's borders who had been severely oppressed during Sunni Ali's reign, feared that his son would continue the harsh policies against them. They made several efforts to try to convince him to become a true Moslem. But the new Songhay emperor rejected these efforts. He refused to let his subjects tell him what he should do.

A group of Moslems organized and decided to overthrow the new king. The revolutionary forces were headed by one of Sunni Ali's own lieutenants. His name was *Askia Muhammad Touré* (as-kee-ah mu-ham-mad too-ray). "Askia" is believed to be a military title. Askia Muhammad was a Soninke. Unlike the Sunni kings, he was a devout Moslem.

The clash between the armies of Askia and the king came in 1493, barely six months after the new king had come to the Songhay throne. At first the king's army, taking advantage of their superior numbers, drove Askia and his men back to a village on the outskirts of Gao. There the rebels rallied and turned on their enemies. The king's forces were routed and he fled south to live the rest of his life in a small village.

Askia Muhammad I ascended the throne of Songhay, the first ruler of a new Askia dynasty. The Moslems of Songhay were overjoyed. They filled the pages of their history books with glowing praise for Askia Muhammad. In one book he was described this way:

"One cannot find his like among those who preceded him nor among those who came after him. He had a lively affection for the doctors, holy persons, and students. He gave much alms . . . and undertook special religious devotions. Full of respect for the doctors, he distributed . . . wealth to them generously to assure the interest of the Moslems and to help them in their submission to God and in the practice of their faith. He caused all the bloody cruelties, iniquities, and faulty innovations introduced by the Sunni to disappear. He established religion (Islam) on the most solid basis."

The Moslems had found a new Songhay ruler much to their liking. The learned doctors, lawyers, and students returned from Walata to resettle in Timbuktu. Askia Muhammad surrounded himself with them, consulted them and honored them.

Oddly enough the Askia restored Ammar to the governorship of Timbuktu, the same Ammar who had plotted with Sunni Ali in the battle of Timbuktu many years before.

ASKIA'S HAJJ

As ruler of the most powerful empire of his time in the western Sudan, Askia Muhammad considered it his

The Songhay emperor, Askia Muhammad made a journey to Mecca in 1495. He was accompanied by 500 horsemen and 1000 foot soldiers. He also took 300,000 pieces of gold with him.

sacred duty to spread Islam throughout the regions under his command. He saw himself as the "Renewer of the Faith." First, he sought to renew his own faith by making the holy pilgrimage to Mecca.

Askia Muhammad set off on his hajj in 1495. He left his brother behind to take care of the affairs of empire while he was away.

The Songhay emperor was accompanied by five hundred horsemen and one thousand foot soldiers on his trip. The Askia also took 300,000 pieces of gold with him. One third of that amount was reserved for the distribution of alms (gifts) in the holy cities of Mecca and Medina and for the support of a shelter in Mecca for Sudanese pilgrims. Another third was to be used to pay the traveling expenses of the emperor and his party. The final third was to be spent on purchases.

During his hajj Askia Muhammad had an audience with the Caliph of Egypt, who solemnly appointed the Askia his lieutenant in Songhay country. The appointment was sealed by placing a bonnet and a turban on Askia's head.

Askia Muhammad returned to his country after an absence of two years. He came back strengthened in faith and glorying in the title of *al Hajj*, the pilgrim. From all accounts Askia Muhammad's generosity on his pilgrimage came close to matching that of Mansa Musa two and a half centuries earlier. Yet the Askia caused less of a stir. By this time, many people had come to expect Sudanese emperors to be rich and generous.

THE HOLY WARS

Askia Muhammad regarded himself as the head and prince of all Moslems in the Sudan. He tried to set a personal example for all Moslems through his own faith and worship. He undertook a series of *jihads* (jee-hads), or holy wars, to bring the Islamic faith to the kingdoms where the people continued to worship the ancient gods. Askia Muhammad began to extend the frontiers of his empire. In the west he gained control of much of the territory that once was part of Mali's empire. In the south he struck against the Mossi kingdom bordering Songhay. The victorious Askia took many of the Mossi children as captives. These youngsters were reared as Moslems. Many of them grew up to become the best soldiers in the Songhay army.

The Askia also led his armies eastward to places where even the Mansas of Mali and Sunni Ali Ber had not ventured. At about 1513, Askia Muhammad's forces swung toward the *Hausa* (how-zah) states, a group of kingdoms between the Niger River and Lake Chad. Hausa towns fell to him one after another. Only the Hausa city of *Kano* (kan-no) put up stiff resistance. This resistance was strong enough to tie up the Songhay army for a year. When Kano finally surrendered, Askia Muhammad once more demonstrated Songhay respect for brave opponents. He permitted the King of Kano to retain his throne. The Askia even gave one of his daughters in marriage to the ruler of Kano.

Now Askia Muhammad was ready to put an end to the dangers of constant raids on Songhay's northeast frontiers by the nomadic Tuaregs. From newly acquired bases in the Hausa states, the Askia led his forces against the Tuareg base in the region of Air. He took the city, drove the Tuaregs into the desert, and founded a colony of Songhay settlers to hold the city. This Negro settlement in the midst of Berber country survives to this day.

Askia Muhammad is remembered for his great ability to govern. He organized a strong central government directly responsible to the king. His rule brought order and prosperity to Songhay.

The Askia's only military setback came at the hands of Kanta, the King of Kebbi (a small kingdom located between the Hausa states and the Niger). Kanta was once allied with the Askia and accompanied the Songhay emperor on his campaigns in Hausa and in Air. But Kanta became upset when he failed to get as large a share of the spoils as he had hoped. So he secured himself behind the walls of the capital of Kebbi and successfully defied the powers of the Askia.

Nevertheless, Askia Muhammad is remembered for his great achievements in unifying a huge area of land. Whereas the empire of Sunni Ali Ber remained largely a confederation of individual states all paying allegiance to the Songhay emperor, the Askia took central government in the western Sudan yet another step.

He appointed governors to each of his provinces. In addition he organized a central government of ministers directly responsible to the king. This ministry included a treasurer, the chief of the navy (of the Songhay canoe fleet), chief tax collector, and chiefs of forests, woodcutters, and fishermen. Each town or large village was governed by a person appointed by the king.

To strengthen the Moslem faith throughout his empire, the Askia appointed Islamic judges to every large district to administer Moslem justice in place of the traditional laws. His own court became the highest court and it heard appeals from the lower courts.

By this time Songhay had become a huge empire characterized by order and prosperity. The vigor of commercial and scholarly activities in the empire served as tributes to the skill and wisdom of Askia the Great.

THE FINAL TRAGEDIES

For all of his accomplishments, Askia Muhammad's last years were filled with misery and despair. One of his own sons led a palace revolt against the aging Askia. By then he was nearly ninety years old and reportedly blind. The Askia was forced to give up the throne. For a time, he was exiled to an island on the Niger where he was plagued by animals and insects. Later the old king was brought back to Gao to live his final days as almost a guest in his own palace. Askia Muhammad died in 1538.

Askia's sons followed each other on the throne. Their misrule helped to hasten the end of the Songhay Empire. By taking advantage of the confusion in the ruling house at Gao, some of the strong states broke away from the control of the Songhay Empire.

The major threat to Songhay came from Morocco. The people there had long profited from the trans-

Saharan gold-salt trade. They reasoned that their profits might be even greater if they controlled both the sources of the salt and the Sudanese gold.

In 1585 the Sultan of Morocco easily snatched the salt mines at Taghaza away from the Songhay Empire. Five years later he sent an army to attack Songhay itself. This army was commanded by a Spaniard who had been taken captive by the Moors when he was only an infant and reared at the royal palace. His name was *Judar Pasha* (ju-dah pah-shah).

Judar's army was small, numbering perhaps only some four thousand fighting men. But his troops were handpicked, highly trained, and equipped with the finest weapons the sultan's money could buy. At least half of the army was armed with weapons newly introduced to West Africa, firearms imported from England.

Though the defending forces of the Songhay far outnumbered the invaders, their swords, spears, and arrows proved no match for the gunfire of the attackers. Gao fell to the invaders, and then Timbuktu surrendered. Judar's army suffered heavy losses, but in the end the superior firepower of the Moors won the day.

The Moors failed to accomplish the main purpose of their invasion. They too had no luck whatever in their attempts to find the source of the Sudanese gold. The sultan died in 1603. His successors decided that the Moorish hold on Songhay was more trouble than it was worth. By 1618, Morocco had lost all interest in its project to turn Songhay into a Moorish colony.

But the Moorish occupation of the important cities of Songhay did not end for another century and a half.

The leaders of the invading Moorish army, left to fend for themselves, soon took over as petty tyrants. They spent most of their time quarreling with one another. Songhay's highly-developed agriculture and commerce went into a decline in the confusion. Once-thriving cities and towns fell into ruin.

In the words of a contemporary Sudanese historian, "From that moment on, everything changed. Danger took the place of security; poverty of wealth. Peace gave way to distress, disasters, and violence."

As the seventeenth century wore on, the Songhay Empire crumbled and disintegrated. The golden era in the history of the western Sudan had come to its end.

The decline of Songhay was hastened by the defeats of its army by the Moors. While the Songhay army had spears and arrows, the Moors had firearms.

CONCLUSION

The Past Shapes the Present

After the disintegration of the Songhay Empire, the power in the Sudan passed to the states of the central Sudan, Hausa, Bornu, and Kanem, to list just a few of them. None of these kingdoms, however, were able to achieve the level of power and splendor attained by Ghana, Mali, and Songhay before them.

Indeed, between the sixteenth and the nineteenth centuries, much of Africa was to go through one of the cruelest experiences that mankind anywhere has had to bear.

The discovery of America had opened vast new lands to exploration and colonization. There came a growing demand for cheap labor to work the plantations of the New World.

European merchants and sailors had established trading posts along the coasts of Africa. Content at first to trade for gold, ivory, and spices, they now discovered something more profitable, the buying of African Negroes for sale as slaves in the Americas. A smart merchant could turn a cargo of human flesh into profits of up to 5000 percent above costs. Some of these merchants showed little concern that their evil business resulted in human suffering and horrors beyond description.

Before the slaving era ended, tens of millions of Negroes from Africa had been packed aboard filthy overcrowded slaving ships and transported across the ocean. Many did not complete their journey. Starvation, neglect, and outright murder took many of them. Eventually some people revolted against the brutal slave trade and it was outlawed throughout the British Empire in 1807. Gradually other nations followed suit. (The story of the slave trade is told more fully in a separate volume of this series.)

Through the slave period, few Europeans penetrated into the interior of the African continent. But this was to change in the nineteenth century. The "industrial revolution" had begun in Europe, and many of the major European lands turned to large-scale manufacturing. New sources of raw materials were needed to feed the new and growing factories of Europe. By this time most of the colonies of the New World had broken away from their European "mother countries." Europe turned once more to Africa as a great, untapped source of wealth.

First came the explorers, followed closely by the colonizers. Soon, the need for raw materials and new markets for the machine-made products of European factories touched off a race for colonies in Africa. In increasing numbers came the Portuguese, the Spanish, English, Dutch, French, Belgians, and later the Germans and the Italians. Most of Africa was gradually divided among the European powers. Most of the territory that once made up the ancient empires of Ghana, Mali, and Songhay fell to the control of the French. That area came to be called the French Sudan, and was part of a larger area which came to be known as French West Africa.

Before their arrival in force, Europeans knew almost nothing about Africa's past. To many of them, Africa remained the "dark continent." And because they knew so little about Africa and its history, it was easy for them to assume that there was nothing to know.

Added to this were the aftereffects of the slave trade. For centuries Europeans rarely saw Africans except those shackled in chains and torn forcibly from their homelands. The slave masters tried to justify the horrors of slavery by saying that Africans were hardly anything more than "primitive savages" who did not deserve the same standards of human decency as other people. And so, a myth that Africa was "a continent without history" came to be widely accepted.

In our own brief look into West Africa's past, we have seen that highly complex societies existed in West Africa. The civilizations of Ghana, Mali, and Songhay developed for the same reasons that civilizations developed everywhere—trade and commerce and the intermixing of people, customs, and ideas. At the heights of their power, the great earlier kingdoms of West Africa compared favorably with their contemporary counterparts in Europe and Asia.

The stories of ancient Ghana, Mali, and Songhay were parts of a larger story, the history of mankind's struggle to live and develop civilization in all parts of our world. The people of these lands were like mankind everywhere, some of them noble, industrious, and forward-looking; others cruel and destructive. We might, for example, think of Sunni Ali in the same way that we consider the Emperor Napoleon of France. Both were warrior-emperors who conquered vast territories. Like Napoleon, Sunni Ali was a hero to some people, a villain to others. Both left an indelible mark on their own lands, and on history.

Why should we concern ourselves with African history? For Americans, the answer shouldn't be too difficult to find. One tenth of the population of the United States is made up of people of African descent. They too have reason to look back proudly to their cultural heritage in the historic past, not to Greece and Rome, perhaps, as in the cases of many other Americans, but to the great civilizations of West Africa. Unfortunately this aspect has frequently been ignored, or at best skimmed over, in many surveys of world history. The result has been a one-sided, distorted view of the historic contributions of different peoples in the advancement of mankind.

In an even larger context, the importance of Africa's past is reflected in the Africa of the present, and future. Within our own lifetimes, the map of Africa has undergone almost a complete redrawing. Just in recent years, more than thirty new African nations were "born." Today, African countries make up nearly one third of the membership of the United Nations.

Look on a map of Africa today and we find that the names of Ghana and Mali have reappeared. To be sure, the modern nations of Ghana and Mali are not exactly the same as their namesakes. But you can be sure also that the leaders of these two new nations did not select these names by picking them out of a hat. They chose them to symbolize their ties to a great cultural past, in the same way that western countries trace their cultures to the glories of Greece and Rome.

Africa, it has been said, has moved full circle from

a golden age through slavery and a colonial era, and now, to independence. As modern Africa re-enters the mainstream of world developments, it cannot help but exert a growing influence in shaping the course of future world events.

For far too long, the path to understanding Africa has been blocked by barriers of ignorance. Today this situation is gradually changing. Thanks to the work and findings of dedicated historians and scientists, a new awareness of Africa's past has begun. By placing Africa and the Africans in their proper historic perspective, the chances of a fruitful and confident future in the relations between Africans and the other peoples of the world are enormously improved.

The continuing thirst for knowledge about Africa is perhaps best summed up by a proverb that originated in Africa itself, "Not to know is bad, not to wish to know is worse."

INDEX